THE BEAUTIFUL LETDOWN: EYES WIDE OPEN

First edition: 2024

ISBN 978-1-0672523-2-8

First Published in 2024

Beyond The Vale Publishing
www.beyondthevalepublishing.com

THE BEAUTIFUL LETDOWN: EYES WIDE OPEN

By

Mugabe Ratshikuni

This book is dedicated to my son Aamari Ndalo Ratshikuni or Lord Keswick as I have nicknamed him, the best thing that life has given to me, my raison d'etre, my game changer, M'lord.

The Beautiful Letdown is inspired by a song of the same title by the American alternative rock band Switchfoot, who just so happen to be one of my favourite bands. These lyrics from the song epitomise every day living and reality in contemporary South Africa for me, "Ah, easy living, You're not much like Your name

Easy dying, hey, You look just about the same

Would you please take me off Your list?

Easy living, please come on and let me down

We are a beautiful letdown

Painfully uncool

The church of the dropouts

The losers, the sinners, the failures, and the fools

Oh, what a beautiful letdown

Are we salt in the wound?

Hey, let us sing one true tune, yeah."

South Africa is a wondrous oxymoron of a country, a beautiful letdown indeed with immense potential and limitless possibilities, it is a country where the dream has been delayed but not yet fully denied, as reflected in the lives of most ordinary Saffas. The articles and opinion pieces that make up the subject matter of this book are mostly inspired by every day conversations with your average South African, at the pub whilst watching a game of rugby over a Klippies and coke or just enjoying a beer and some shooters with the lads in our pub group of over ten years, over dinner whilst catching up with mates and sipping on a fine selection of fermented grapes from the Western Cape, whilst braaing at a mate's place and engaging in intense debate with strangers that one has just met and immediately hit it off with.

It is the chronicles of post-94 South Africa, a country in a perpetual state of existential crisis, which still radiates the positive energy and joie de vivre of a Freddie Mercury live performance, however. For all of its idiosyncrasies, South Africa remains a country with a certain je ne sais quoi that is profoundly appealing and charming. This book stems from my humble attempt at elevating the public discourse within contemporary South Africa through opinion pieces, articles, and columns. I hope it will contribute positively towards taking the conversation forward in search of creative solutions to our manifold challenges as a country, which solutions would propel us to achieve our developmental aspirations.

The issues we wrestle with on a daily basis as a country are as complex and compelling as the plot in the 2009 movie, Eyes Wide Open, by Director Haim Tabakman, but the vision remains, "Hey, let us sing one true tune, yeah", as some of the lyrics in the Switchfoot song referred to above go. Now you know the inspiration and story behind the title of this book, and I hope you enjoy reading it and it leaves you with more questions than answers.

Mugabe Funzani Ratshikuni

Table of Contents

FOREWORD

"THE BEAUTIFUL LETDOWN: EYES WIDE OPEN": What an apt description of how many South Africans who fought for a brighter future feel at the moment. Even the so-called born-frees were thrust into this new world, post 1994, with promises of a bigger, better, and brighter future for all South Africans, "The Rainbow Nation", that the late Archbishop Desmond Tutu sold to us as a very tangible reality for current and future generations.

I met Mugabe Ratshikuni in 2015 and from our very first conversation, I knew he was different to many other people that I had encountered. Erudite and eloquent in his articulation and thinking, controversial and yet very interesting. A poet of sorts, I came to realise, and a deeply spiritual individual. We engaged on topics ranging from politics, family, God, poetry and even my plans to author a book, amongst a plethora of issues that we delved deeply into. When you come across him the first time, preacher and Bible teacher is certainly not what first comes to mind, so I was pleasantly surprised to find out that he had been a pastor and church leader at a certain point in his life. It is my immense pleasure and honour to have this opportunity to write the foreword for his long-awaited book. I have over the years continued to read many of his writings, which he constantly posts on LinkedIn. He remains deeply thoughtful and engaging whilst sticking to being provocative in his commentary.

Mine is a very complex and complicated background, starting off as an Accountant & Auditor, to being a Corporate Financier, then an Equity Analyst, and after that a Government Official to finally ending up as an entrepreneur. It is therefore quite daunting to write a foreword for a book written by someone who is not very conventional and is a contrarian of note, as I imagine many people would see me as conservative and perhaps conformist, but here we go.

The brief that I was given was to write a three-to-five-page foreword for this book. I struggled with the idea of what to say for five pages without waffling. I was reminded of my late father's words, which are as follows, "when you speak for too long, you are being disrespectful to your audience. Keep it succinct and to the point in order to deliver the key message so that it lands as it should." This wise counsel from my late father informed my brevity in preparing this foreword, despite the breadth and depth of the subject matter that is covered in this book.

In his many intellectual musings, Mugabe has found a fine balance between intellectual critique and self-deprecation. This makes it easy to absorb and appreciate his articles. Despite the great depth of his articles, he has somehow found a way to make very complex concepts accessible to the ordinary, unsophisticated reader with his laid-back, sociable and very conversational writing style. One cannot go through the material in this book and be left in any doubt that one is indeed being exposed to a brilliant mind.

Having said that, I'm not sure that I agree with all of his assertions in the book, most specifically his commendation of Hendrik Verwoerd's intellectual prowess, but the point of all good writing of this nature is not necessarily to solicit agreement, but rather to stimulate discussion and debate and encourage critical reasoning and thinking within public discourse. On the Verwoerd matter, my sense is that any person of reputable intellect would have known that the apartheid project was not sustainable and was bound to fail eventually. A highly intelligent person would have rather utilised their intellectual ability to build a more equitable society for future generations and not one that would lead a whole nation to an existential crisis, as we remain with the socio-economic challenges that were brought about and perpetuated by his brainchild, the apartheid system. On this point, Mugabe and I clearly have different perspectives.

Mugabe clearly has many conversations with diverse people from disparate corners of the country, who all have very interesting views about our economy and the pertinent yet thorny issue of transformation. His weaving these conversations into his articles exposes us to a much more robust view of the world as seen by ordinary South Africans, and not just what we are fed by various media platforms.

Some of his articles seem to be at odds with each other in my view, which is not a bad thing from where I am sitting as it again reflects the current state of mind of many South Africans, who one day subscribe to a particular view on a matter of economic importance depending on how we're faring economically at that point in time, only to later on take on a very different view when circumstances change. By way of example, he posits in one article that due to our past, we need to have a developmental state that intervenes across the broad spectrum of our economy to bring transformation and economic growth in order to achieve equality amongst all races. In another instance, within the context of experiencing load shedding, he posits that we should privatise state-owned entities as they are inefficient and in fact, state ownership might hamper our ability to achieve equality across all races. These wavering sentiments are a true reflection of our state as a nation, which calls into question the responsiveness of our economic policies to the lived experiences of our populace. He does, however, later on, call for balance through a partnership model between the state and the private sector. So, which one is it abeg? (As our West African brothers and sisters would posit this very pertinent question).

A typical human being changes their mind all the time. Some may see this as being a political or intellectual prostitute, or perhaps a chameleon to be kinder. I, however, hold the firm view that no intellectual can hold a singular view regardless of the shifting sands of life as it were. So again, Mugabe and I seem to agree but also disagree, which I believe to be a healthy state of existence.

As a proponent of gender and racial economic transformation, I have followed very closely the debates around black economic empowerment and the contrast with the Afrikaner empowerment model of yesteryear.

In an article I penned in August 2008 which was published by IOL, I posited the following: "Afrikaner empowerment is a powerful model for today". I argued as follows: Sanlam/Santam, Absa, Naspers, BHP Billiton, Pepkor, Venfin, Remgro and KWV are all companies that are examples of highly successful businesses started by Afrikaner entrepreneurs during the height of Afrikaner nationalism under apartheid.

Afrikaner empowerment history makes for interesting reading. It reminds one that it is possible to turn around the economic fortunes of previously marginalised peoples as the Afrikaners did after obtaining political emancipation when the National Party came to power in 1948. At the time, more than seventy per cent of Afrikaners were rural and involved in agriculture. Commerce and industry were dominated by English-speaking white people and the Indian and Jewish communities.

The Afrikaner concentration in farming resulted in the government providing financial incentives to bolster that sector's performance, ensuring Afrikaners had access to significant amounts of capital. When they started moving into commerce and industry, there was also a fairly significant "toenadering" (drawing together) by the Afrikaner community, which involved setting up the financing institutions that funded many successful Afrikaner entrepreneurial ventures. All these efforts were bolstered by the 1939 National Economic Conference, of which one key outcome was the decision to launch an economic movement that would harness the Afrikaner community's resources to develop an Afrikaner capitalist class.

The driving force was the desire for self-determination by the Afrikaner people. The conference decided on several measures to improve Afrikaners' economic position within SA society. Amongst these were the provision of commercial and technical training for Afrikaner youth; the mobilisation of Afrikaner capital and savings for investment; and the setting up of agricultural and commercial co-operatives as well as Afrikaans cultural organisations. The Afrikaners were unapologetic in pursuing a capitalist developmental agenda for themselves driven by the state. This unrelenting stance led to the Afrikaner community's prominence in the local economy. Helped by the government in putting pressure on English-dominated corporate South Africa, Afrikaners amassed resources to dominate the economy.

One can argue of course that we have had 30 years to not only emulate but even improve on the Afrikaner empowerment model. But alas! We are now contending with not just state capture, but the construction mafia and many other situations of malfeasance in our society brought onto us by ourselves sadly. All of these things have only had the effect of denying us Africans the potential to realise our "African Dream" as beautifully sung by Vicky Simpson or put differently, the former President of the African Development Bank ("AfDB") Dr Ronald Kabureka once asked a pertinent question at the 2015 African Development Bank Annual meeting in Rwanda when he said, "I hear Africa is rising, but for whom"? The germane question of course is whether it is rising for Africans or for our erstwhile Western colonisers or our impending Eastern Colonisers?

Mugabe's poignant comment about "The Beautiful Letdown: Eyes Wide Open" is a rather sad lamentation similar to the lyrics by the renowned artist Selimo Thabane where he sings "Kotsi ea mahlomola." We continue to be confronted with the imminent danger of disaster as a nation if we do not take care to take corrective action spiritually, politically, and holistically. The vexing issue for South Africans remains that, "Re phuthile matshoho, re shebilie banna ha ba sebetsa," as aptly put by Sankomota, the legendary eighties group coming out of the Mountain Kingdom of Lesotho.

Mohau Polo Leteka

October 2024

Mohau Polo Leteka is many things. A mother, a daughter, a sibling, a lover of all things fine and wonderful, a believer in a higher being, a lover of people, a daughter of the most High God, a pathfinder and a social activist. Others call her an entrepreneur and investor. Take your pick.

She is the Founder and CEO of IDF Capital, which has contributed significantly to the empowerment of women within the mainstream economy through channelling investments into women-owned high-growth entrepreneurial businesses across sub-Saharan Africa. She is also the Co-Founder of Agooji, a Pan African investment company that invests in women-owned and women-run businesses across Sub-Saharan Africa as well as a founder of the I'M IN Accelerator which focuses on launching black and women-owned, high-growth start-ups into the African technology sector.

She is the current President of the Association for Black Securities and Investment Professionals (ABSIP) a position she has held since 2020. She holds a Master's degree in International Business with Law from the University of Salford where her dissertation focussed on how to implement and practically operationalise the Africa Continental Free Trade Agreement.

1

IT'S THE ECONOMY, STUPID

Land Expropriation without Compensation Critical to Addressing the Land Issue in South Africa

In the introduction to Cedric Nunn's, Unsettled: One Hundred Years War of Resistance by Xhosa against Boer and British, renowned South Africa author and intellectual Zakes Mda makes the following poignant observation about the historic relationship that the African people have always had with the land which they lived in and what it means to them, *"these landscapes are storage places of memory. Embedded in these rocks, these dongas, these trees, these hills, these rivers, these valleys, these ruins, these monuments, these cities, these cairns are generations of narratives that continue to haunt the present."*

The question of land dispossession and land reform has been one that has not been adequately addressed in the post-1994 dispensation and the recent huge uproar concerning the ANC's decision at its 54th national conference to push for a policy of land expropriation without compensation, a position which parliament has also adopted, has highlighted the fact that the land issue is highly emotive for people on all sides of the divide.

As Zakes Mda so aptly puts it, for the African people who were dispossessed unjustly of their land by the colonialists, the land issue is a deeply held scar that needs to be addressed with urgency because land for them is deeply ingrained into their identity, their sense of being and worth, their social and economic organisation.

That is why we must resolve the land question if we want to succeed in our nation-building objectives. Historically, the forced removals and dispossession of land from Africans, have left them impoverished and disempowered, with the effects of that dastardly act still being felt in present-day South Africa.

As the ANC-led government, we want to use the agricultural sector, with its forward and backward linkages to drive modernisation, industrialisation, transformation, job creation, food security, economic inclusion, and equality.

This means that our posture to expropriate land without compensation to redress the injustices of the past is a necessary act in building a more just, equitable and inclusive society. Of course, this expropriation will be done in a manner that is constitutional and that will allow us to ensure that there is sufficient land for social and economic development, to effect radical and spatial transformation to redress past injustices.

Our land reform programme will not just be haphazard, and as we expropriate without compensation we will ensure that we adhere to the principles of increased security of tenure, land redistribution, and land restitution. Our focus will primarily be on vacant land, unused and underutilised land as well as land held for speculation and hopelessly indebted land.

So, our approach to land expropriation without compensation will not be a helter-skelter, scatter-gunned approach. We will apply constitutional principles and be sure to promote the public benefit (not just that of an elite few) in how we roll out the land reform programme. The final aim will be to vest the land of our country as the common property of the people of South Africa as a whole for their communal benefit.

This means that markets, investors, farmers, and all other relevant stakeholders need not be afraid of land expropriation without compensation. A more inclusive economy, with ownership of land and other assets more equitably spread out, can only be to the benefit of the economy and the country as a whole going forward.

Right at the heart of our economic transformation and economic justice agenda, is this critical land reform programme. Let us reverse the apartheid and colonial legacy of forced removals (in urban areas but also from ancestral lands in rural areas which were unjustly allocated to White farmers and White owners). Let us reverse the legacy of alienation from their land that black people felt when the migrant labour system forced them to leave their rural land and go into the cities to sell their labour for the sake of upholding an unjust economic system. Let us support land expropriation without compensation as an existential necessity for the growth, development and safeguarding of our young, dynamic, vibrant, and maturing democracy.

It is only in getting behind such a progressive land reform programme that we will be able to defeat the phenomenon of black disempowerment and marginalisation that Sol Plaatje so profoundly describes in his editorial to the Bechuana Gazette in 1902, *"I am Black but comely, O ye daughters of Jerusalem, as the tents of Kedar and the curtains of Solomon. Look not upon me because I am Black for the sun hath looked upon me; my mother's children were angry with me; they made me the keeper of their vineyards; but my own vineyards have I not kept."* It is only by giving our people back the land that we will be able to ensure that they become "keepers of their own vineyards" as opposed to those of others.

VBS and the Quest for Radical Socio-economic Transformation

The recent furore around VBS Bank and the South African Reserve Bank (SARB) putting it under curatorship, after the bank accepted deposits from municipalities which it is not legally permitted to do under the Municipal Finance Management Act of 2003, brought to the fore the critical challenges that we are faced with as a country in our quest for radical socio-economic transformation aimed at bringing black people and historically disadvantaged individuals and communities into meaningful mainstream economic activity as well as transforming racially skewed ownership patterns that prevent our economy from growing inclusively.

In discussing this issue with a very close mate of mine who is in the financial services sector, notwithstanding the merits of the SARB's actions, we ended up focussing on the critical matter of how to transform the various sectors of our economy, which still remain largely owned and controlled by a few, large, elite firms across entire value chains. These firms, of course, for historically obvious reasons are mostly owned and controlled by white people (it wouldn't be contemporary South Africa if every issue didn't end up at some point boiling down to race, would it?)

My mate's main argument in beginning this debate was to say that we black South Africans need to start building our own businesses, independent of the state if we want to see genuine transformation which will help us grow economically as well as fight income and asset (wealth) inequality.

My quick response to this was to highlight the fact that the Afrikaner banks of the apartheid era, which are amongst the mainstream banking establishment at present, as well as most of the big Afrikaaner conglomerates that now make up a large part of mainstream corporate South Africa, were indeed started with the assistance and support of the National Party government and so there is nothing wrong with Black business and the state deliberately working together to transform our economy through building and investing in capacity by being preferential to each other.

Perhaps (as in this case), what we need to do is to relook and rework some of the laws which were put in place for good reasons, but hinder us in our quest to see a more transformed, inclusive economy I argued. After all, Black business and Black businesspeople do not have the same access to social capital (and all its benefits) that White business and White people do and as such government must be systematic, unapologetic, and very intentional about empowering, supporting, developing, and promoting (pushing) Black business across all sectors of our economy I further argued. Doing so, would contrary to popular, mainstream opinion, not lower standards or contribute to corruption, but would rather further our developmental objectives as a nation.

Of course, in saying so, I am fully aware that not all Black businesses are innately progressive and transformational in their inclination, nature, ethos, and objectives. My thinking was highly influenced by French Sociologist Pierre Bourdieu's book, Distinction: A Social Critique of the Judgement of Taste.

Bourdieu's classical work could be used to infer that social capital plays a determining role in enabling people within society to access resources that are important to succeed, through social networks or institutionalised relationships. In fact, taking this a step further, social capital, it could be argued allows people access to economic capital, not only because of what they know (and are capable of) but added to that also who they know.

In line with this thinking, one of the biggest problems that any black person(s) or business is faced with, is that for historically obvious reasons, they don't have access to the critical social capital that is required to succeed within a corporate space or as a business person, hence you find that most black businesses struggle with funding for their businesses, access to markets in a highly monopolised economy controlled by a connected few (which are some of the barriers to entry that keep our economy from being truly transformed).

As a result of this, the government must be deliberate and radical about giving black people and black businesses opportunities. This is not corruption, but an important intervention in breaking the social capital barrier that makes success difficult for black people and black businesses.

In a world that works on networking and networks, it is actually an insult to insinuate that when black people get given opportunities, it is nepotism whereas when whites do it, we call it using their networks. It is the same thinking that makes people label those blacks who do business with the government derogatively as tenderpreneurs, when a large chunk of government business goes to big, established private sector companies in fact, and they are called legitimate, genuine enterprises. The same thinking informs the labelling of anything untoward that has to do with black business as corruption when similar behaviour by big, mostly white-owned corporations is reduced to mere collusion.

The point here is that we need to stop being so emotional and emotive about such issues and realise that we are still dealing with a huge backlog from our divided past and we need specific, targeted interventions by the government and other role players to level the playing field.

Doing so does not equate to racism or favouring one race at the expense of another unjustly, but rather it is a critical nation-building imperative as we pursue inclusive economic growth. After all, it was renowned author Malcolm Gladwell in his highly celebrated book Outliers who made a similar point by highlighting the fact that no one comes from poverty and rises up the ladder to make it on their own. Their success is built on advantages, opportunities, and networks that they accumulate through life (some deserved, some not so deserved), so that in the end what we call an outlier in life is not that much of an outlier after all.

Monopolies are a Bottleneck to Development

Over the past weekend, whilst busy researching and analysing the investment climate in Gauteng (since investment is one of the main buzzwords of the "New Dawn", one must try and get a better understanding of the outlook), I happened to pick up an old book, that I read in my days as a young student, Robert Tressell's perennially axiomatic novel, The Ragged Trousered Philanthropists.

Of course, once I opened the book, I couldn't put it down and was completely engrossed in it until I finished it. While devouring this book, I was drawn to reflect once again on the ills that continue to hold us back as a country: poverty, inequality, economic exclusion, what causes these ills and why we are still struggling to overcome them and they are seemingly getting worse over two decades into our democratic dispensation.

A very long quote from the book struck me as poignant and pertinent in this regard, "Poverty is not caused by men and women getting married; it's not caused by machinery; it's not caused by "over-production"; it's not caused by drink or laziness; and it's not caused by "over-population". It's caused by Private Monopoly.

That is the present system. They have monopolised everything that it is possible to monopolise; they have got the whole earth, the minerals in the earth and the streams that water the earth. The only reason they have not monopolised the daylight and the air is that it is not possible to do it. If it were possible to construct huge gasometers and to draw together and compress within them the whole of the atmosphere, it would have been done long ago, and we should have been compelled to work for them to get money to buy air to breathe.

 And if that seemingly impossible thing were accomplished tomorrow, you would see thousands of people dying for want of air - or of the money to buy it - even as now thousands are dying for want of the other necessities of life. You would see people going about gasping for breath, and telling each other that the likes of them could not expect to have air to breathe unless they had the money to pay for it.

Most of you here, for instance, would think and say so. Even as you think at present that it's right for so few people to own the Earth, the Minerals and the Water, which are all just as necessary as the air. In the same spirit as you now say: "It's Their Land," "It's Their Water," "It's Their Coal," "It's Their Iron," so you would say "It's Their Air," "These are their gasometers, and what right have the likes of us to expect them to allow us to breathe for nothing?"

And even while he is doing this the air monopolist will be preaching sermons on the Brotherhood of Man; he will be dispensing advice on "Christian Duty" in the Sunday magazines; he will give utterances to numerous more or less moral maxims for the guidance of the young. And in the meantime, all around, people will be dying for want of some of the air that he will have bottled up in his gasometers.

And when you are all dragging out a miserable existence, gasping for breath or dying for want of air, if one of your number suggests smashing a hole in the side of one of the gasometers, you will all fall upon him in the name of law and order, and after doing your best to tear him limb from limb, you'll drag him, covered with blood, in triumph to the nearest Police Station and deliver him up to "justice" in the hope of being given a few half-pounds of air for your trouble."

The staggering reality of the South African situation is that we keep upholding a system that is structured in such a manner that it benefits the few at the expense of the many. The economy is still structured in a manner that a few large firms control entire value chains at the expense of competition, small business development and entrepreneurship, innovation and inclusive growth.

It is these big monopolies that still own and control our economy, as Robert Tressell's The Ragged Trousered Philanthropists so aptly highlights, that are keeping us from achieving our developmental goals. A developmental state should be looking at breaking the power of these monopolies, by creating an opportunity for new entrants to shake up the economy and introduce greater competition and competitiveness.

The problem, as Professor Steven Friedman highlighted a couple of years ago, is that, as much as most business leaders are aware that our economy is not open and inclusive enough (and hence keeps the majority on the periphery), they are wont to resist any change as it might cause them to pay a higher price than they are willing to.

It is much easier to blame the unions and government, without taking responsibility for the fact that it is big business and the monopoly that they hold over most sectors of our economy that is a true bottleneck to progress in our country.

The whole system is geared towards defending the interests of those who already hold the levers of the economy, even at the expense of a developmental agenda and inclusive growth. To say so, does not make one a socialist or a "commie" as some would like to fallaciously label one (I, myself am not an ideologue in that sense just for the record). To say so does not make one "anti-business", but rather pro-development and economic inclusivity.

The high levels of protest and unrest within the country are a sign, not just of government failure in delivering services as some amongst us would have us believe, but rather of a social compact gone wrong, of a people that are frustrated and increasingly angry at being left out in the cold economically, a people that are experiencing the haunting reality so brilliantly described by African American intellectual W.E.B Du Bois, "To be a poor man is hard, but to be a poor race in a land of dollars is the very bottom of hardships."

So, in order to positively move forward as a country, we must break the status quo across all segments of society, we must make the necessary sacrifices to enhance and promote economic inclusivity. This requires that big business and these private monopolies that dominate our economy be broken down so that we can increase competitiveness and innovation within our economy. To not do so, would be tantamount to committing economic suicide of the highest order which will derail, if not completely dismantle the nation-building agenda. In Robert Tressell's words, "Every man who is not helping to bring about a better state of affairs for the future is helping to perpetuate the present misery and is therefore the enemy of his own children. There is no such thing as being neutral: we must either help or hinder."

The South African Dream

A few years ago, I read a very interesting book which will provide the background and the substance of this week's article. The book concerned was titled, **The South African Dream**, co-authored by two brilliant South African entrepreneurs, John Hunt and Reg Lascaris of TBWA/Hunt/Lascaris fame. The main aim of the book was to try to construct and articulate some sort of South African Dream which would inspire us as a nation and serve as a driver to South Africa fulfilling its immense potential. Looking at the many challenges that we are faced with as a nation, I was reminded of this book, over the past week and I decided that my next article would be aimed at constructing and articulating a "South African Dream."

It was the poet Langston Hughes who said, "Hold fast to dreams. For if dreams die, life is a broken-winged bird that cannot fly." Dreams are important because the ability to dream is a prerequisite for the ability to achieve and if South Africa as a nation is ever going to fulfil its potential, we will need a well-articulated dream which we can all work towards as a people. According to Hunt and Lascaris, both advertising industry legends, "the commercial marketplace is built on dreams. Dreams define who we are and who we want to become. Dreams are not an intangible, wishy-washy issue. Advertisers and marketers don't sell products, they sell dreams. Show understanding of individual aspirations or show how a product fits into a consumer's imagined, ideal lifestyle and you are close to clinching the sale." In other words, whatever dream we are trying to sell to the South African populace to build a winning nation, must be a dream that fits into the imagined, ideal, lifestyle of the average South African. A survey conducted a few years back found that there was strong agreement across all racial groups in South Africa with the following statements:

1) Hard work will get me where I need to go in life.

2) Competition makes me perform better and feels more rewarding in the end.

3) What I do affects what comes to me in the end.

4) I like the fact that achieving my goals will take effort on my part.

From the above-mentioned statements we can deduce that the South African dream must incorporate the values of hard work, competition or competitiveness, pro-activeness, and self-drive or initiative. So, what is the South African Dream then? Well in my view the South Dream is four-fold, or it can be divided into four aspects. Firstly, the dream entails a renewed focus on **entrepreneurship and entrepreneurs**. In the words of Robbie Brozin, the founder/owner of Nandos, "South Africa has had a political miracle, we shouldn't be greedy, but we need a business miracle to match. Everybody must do their bit by becoming entrepreneurial, by contributing to economic activity, by building and creating their opportunities."

We have a population that believes in hard work and in taking risks, that prefers to run its own businesses, that wants to try something new and that thinks competition leads to superior performance. We must develop entrepreneurial skills. We have to mobilise individuals and become a society that welcomes and values new ideas. This is why our diversity as a nation is such a positive factor. The greater the number of contributors, the greater the chance of coming up with new business solutions. Diversity leads to more creative ideas. Entrepreneurship is the solution to the problems of joblessness, homelessness, and crime that South Africa faces.

In the words of Clem Sunter, "Joblessness is more fundamental than homelessness, because if a man has a job he can buy a house. Joblessness is one of the chief sources of crime. So, if you can reduce joblessness, you automatically have an impact on crime." To create this entrepreneurial class in our country we need to create easier access to capital for budding entrepreneurs. We need new thinking and new attitudes from financiers and venture capitalists. We need new, context-specific financing models from banks and financiers if entrepreneurship is going to flourish in South Africa. We also need to modernise township economies, because that is where most of this entrepreneurial class should come from. We need fresh attitudes and fresh ideas from the formal sector that will take the informal trading activities and entrepreneurial energy that is prevalent in the townships of South Africa and bring all that into the formal economy. As a nation, we need to make the entrepreneur a hero. Our education system needs to shift from just simply focusing on mass-producing employees and "employable" graduates to focusing on producing more pioneers, entrepreneurs, and business owners. To use the words of Theodor Roethke, "What we need are more people who specialise in the impossible."

Secondly, the South African Dream needs to focus on a **renewal of morality and work ethic**. The words of Oscar Wilde are pertinent in this regard, "our ambition should be to rule ourselves, the true kingdom for each of us, and true progress is to know more and be more." We should promote and celebrate self-governance as a nation. Instead of creating a society that is highly reliant on external governance, we need to encourage our people to learn, to grow into self-leadership and self-governance. This will help solve a lot of the socio-economic problems that seem to hamper us as a nation, for example, for all the talk about the government's failure in the battle against HIV/AIDS, the sad reality is that the reason for the prevalence of HIV/AIDS in South Africa is that a large part of the population has no self-governance when it comes to the area of their sexuality and they then blame government when they fall prey to HIV/AIDS and all its destructive socio-economic effects.

We need to answer the question that was posed by Hunt and Lascaris, "Are we grubby materialists, high idealists or a bit of both? Reveal the dream and the nation itself stands revealed." In trying to answer this question as we define the South African Dream, we need to remind ourselves that a noble calling and the call of self-interest are not of necessity mutually exclusive. For too many in South Africa, it appears that the South African Dream is to milk the system and get something for nothing. This kind of attitude needs to be discouraged in favour of a higher morality and a better work ethic. We need to promote genuine moral regeneration as a key part of the South African Dream. In the words of former president, Nelson Mandela, "As we reconstruct the material conditions of our existence, we must also change our way of thinking; to respect the value and result of honest work, and to treat each law of the country as our own. This is our call to all South Africans to firm up the moral fibre of our nation. It is a call to artists and musicians and sports persons, to religious leaders and traditional institutions, to intellectuals, to the media and to all those who should give leadership as we establish new symbols and role models; all of us to join hands in a new patriotism, not because the government says so, but because it is in our common interest to do it."

We need to create an open, transparent society that treats everybody fairly; where things are done on merit and competence instead of being decided by the kind of low-level politics we have seen in South Africa. A lot of the corruption that we see could be halted by simply removing temptation and substituting sensible controls in South African society. The South African Dream in this regard is mostly about opportunities which allow people to progress in accordance with the skills, talent, and ambition they have. Key areas to sort out to bring this about would be education, health, and the family.

Thirdly, the South African dream has a **political focus**. We need higher levels of literacy with more people reading which will ensure a more informed citizenry which in turn will strengthen democracy. We need to create a society that places more confidence in our democratic institutions and systems, than in individual politicians and political organisations. We need to promote a greater level of participation by the citizenry in our democratic institutions. We need to instil a greater commitment to democracy and transparency in the average South African.

Finally, the South African Dream has an **African and a global dimension**. Here I appeal to the words of a South African political heavyweight, a Nobel peace laureate and a former ANC president, Chief Albert Luthuli, in his 1962 book: Let My People Go, "the task is not finished. South Africa is not yet a home for all her sons and daughters. Such a home we wish to ensure from the beginning, as history has been one of ascending unities, and the breaking of tribal, racial, and creedal barriers. The past cannot hope to have a life sustained only by itself, wrenched from the whole. There remains before us the building of a new land, a land for, men who are Black, White, brown, from the ruins of the old narrow groups, a synthesis of the rich cultural strains which we have inherited. There remains to be achieved in our integration with the rest of our continent. Somewhere ahead there beckons a civilisation which will take its place in the parade of God's history, besides other great human syntheses: Chinese, Egyptian, Jewish, and European. It will not necessarily be all Black: but it will be African." We must create a competitive spirit which says, "We can beat the world. We can be successful." We need to create a greater openness and awareness of the world for ordinary South Africans so we can take our place and make our contribution to the global family of nations.

This is the South African Dream that I believe should inform our decisions and drive us as a nation. It was the Anglo-Irish poet, William Butler Yeats who said, "In dreams begins responsibility." Our major construct is not money. It is having enough human beings with the appropriate qualities to turn dreams into realities. We need to become a nation of dreamers whose dream motivates them to sacrifice and action. I end off with words from T.E Lawrence (Lawrence of Arabia) in his Seven Pillars of Wisdom, "All men dream, but not equally. Those who dream by night in the dusty recesses of their minds wake in the day to find it was vanity. But the dreamers of the day are dangerous men for they may act out their dreams with open eyes to make it possible." May we be a nation of dangerous dreamers, "dreamers of the day who act out their dreams with open eyes" so that the South African Dream can become a reality in our lifetime.

Exploring Afrikaner Nationalism As A Development Model

I spent the past weekend reading Pieter Du Toit's book, The

Stellenbosch Mafia: Inside the Billionaires Club, a wonderful read which gives one even more perspective and respect for great apartheid-era Afrikaner industrialists such as Rupert and Hertzog.

There are some fascinating insights from the book, which are germane for us as contemporary South Africans trying to chart an inclusive development path going forward. The idea of "volkskapitalisme" (people's capitalism) is one such intriguing insight, which is worth exploring from a developmental perspective, for black South Africans, who remain the most economically disempowered in the current dispensation.

I know my socialist mates from the Alliance partners of the ANC will be livid with me for even making such a suggestion, but contrary to the "comfortable ignorance" of most people on this platform, who automatically brand anything and everyone ANC as "commie/leftie", we are not all Marxists in the ANC folks. I know, it is a bit difficult for some to stomach this truth, but yeah, we are truly a "broad church" as the ANC. These are the kinds of nuances that people who are still stuck in a 1980s-era "rooi gevaar/swart gevaar", binary mode, will never appreciate, so I won't even try convincing anyone any further.

Du Toit's book is brilliant because it makes you appreciate the genius of the Afrikaaner industrialists who took the Afrikaans nation out of poverty, whilst not overlooking and ignoring the historical context within which this happened. He makes the point that Afrikaners controlled no major industrial enterprises at the beginning of the 20th century and constituted a large part of the "poor white problem" in the country, despite dominating the political space. In fact, as Du Toit highlights, Afrikaners played almost no part in the emerging, modernising economy of South Africa at the time. An interesting parallel can be drawn between that and contemporary realities in South Africa.

Also, of great interest to me, is the assertion by Du Toit that Afrikaners at that time, with their nationalist sentiments, were very suspicious of capitalism and capital, something which they of course overcame through time as state-led development facilitated their empowerment and integration into the mainstream economy. Interesting, given those who keep knocking on the new dispensation and its perceived "anti-capital" sentiment. Maybe there is something to be said here about this being a necessary phase of a people's struggle towards economic emancipation, but that's just me with my "limited or non-existent" thinking and critical reasoning capacity, as most readers on this platform have seemingly concluded, attempting to "think out loud", so maybe just dismiss that attempt at a thought.

Du Toit also argues that Afrikaaner business has flourished more after being unshackled from apartheid, citing the post-94 successes of the likes of Naspers, Sanlam, and the emergence of new enterprises such as Jannie Mouton's PSG as pertinent examples. He quotes renowned scenario planner and futurist Clem Sunter, who said, *"The Afrikaaners were liberated by the creation of a level playing field. Necessity is indeed the mother of invention. Entitlement shackles it."*

He argues further, using Sunter as a reference point, that Afrikaners were the real beneficiaries of the democratic dispensation (I know, this is complete rubbish from where you are sitting right?) because democracy meant that Afrikaners lost their privileged position in society and were forced to fend for themselves as they were no longer able to rely on the state and its networks to succeed.

Methinks there might be a huge lesson there for black South Africans, in the struggle for economic participation and emancipation but again, what do I know, being an "entitled, corrupt, lazy, inept" deployed ANC cadre right?

In pursuit of economic emancipation, Afrikaaners founded key institutions such as die Federale Volksbeleggings, which provided venture capital for Afrikaner businesspeople and extended a loan to Dr Anton Rupert to establish die Voorbrand Tobacco Company, upon which the Rupert empire was built. As Du Toit highlights, the state at the time created a protected environment for Afrikaner enterprises to grow and flourish.

Afrikaners also developed their own world-class educational institutions, such as Stellenbosch, and through that, they were able to develop Afrikaans, a beautifully expressive, rich African language (I can already hear you say, jeepers, is this the same "racist cadre" writing here, but I can't be held responsible for your parochial reception and interpretation of my views, based on the political party I proudly belong to) into a language of academia and commerce, an important aspect in the economic migration of any people.

Hence, as I have stated in public before, I see no wrong with Afrikaners looking to build their own schools and institutions in the current dispensation to preserve their language and culture. After all, it is this rich diversity and heritage, which, when celebrated within a nation-building context, makes South Africa a beautiful rainbow. It is this "plurality of centres" as Ngugi wa Thiong'o writes about, which will make South Africa a winning nation.

There is a lesson here for black South Africans, who are looking to integrate and participate meaningfully and significantly within the mainstream South African economy. The challenge for government in our day is to encourage the development of other languages and cultures through native language schools and universities, which will enable those languages and cultures to also become languages of academia and commerce, an important evolution in terms of looking to participate meaningfully in the value chains of any economy as a people.

The other thing Du Toit highlights is the fact that Afrikaaners were looking to grow and develop their own businesses to compete with established English monopolies. They were not looking to take over existing English businesses as part of some "empowerment" scheme. Again, a massive lesson for black business, the likes of the Black Business Council and the Black Management Forum as well as the government's much-maligned Black Industrialist scheme, come to mind here.

A final thought that came to mind, was the part where Du Toit highlights how Nelson Mandela, whilst in prison, took time to study the Afrikaner people and their psyche. There was much about the Afrikaner nation that he admired as a result of that, without in any way of course, condoning the evils of the system that they imposed on South Africa. So, you can learn from and admire certain traits that your "adversary" possesses, without in any way embracing and endorsing their warped ideology. This sheds some light on Mcebo Freedom Dlamini's infamous comments, by the way, but I digress and don't want to spoil a good story (entrenched narrative) by highlighting some simple facts.

I mean, for me to say that I think Hendrik Verwoerd was a brilliant mind (I do, by the way), a historical fact, is not to endorse the evil ideology that he promulgated. Verwoerd was an academic achiever, and a very gifted fellow, which is admirable and noteworthy, just a pity that he didn't use that brilliant mind of his to contribute towards the building of a better South Africa for all, but again, this is just a side issue, which I will end on.

The State and Development

The other day, I was having a conversation with an economist mate of mine from varsity and we ended up discussing how the government operates and the impact this has on the economy.

You see, my economist mate is from the neoliberal school of economics, and he feels that the biggest problem that we have in this country is that the state is trying to drive the economy, whereas in his view it should be business that takes the lead in matters economic, with the state in the background merely playing the role of a referee.

His critique was that our plans to develop the economy, create jobs and materially improve the lives of our citizens are too state-centric. He gave the classical neoliberal riposte that the state and its technocrats should not be dictating the pace and direction of economic development. "How, praytell," he asked, "can government bureaucrats be left to determine which industries should be stimulated in our economy in order to produce the greatest possible growth and development?"

In his view, this is something best left to that nebulous thing called the markets to determine, as markets will by default eliminate those industries which are weak and promote those which are beneficial. He was adamant that we should be sticking to the mantra of "the market knows best" if we want to build a strong economy.

My argument in return, was that what we need is an economic model that will not only produce growth within our economy but in effect will develop and enhance the abilities, and the capacity of those within the state., as opposed to a passive state, which is in the background being led by business, what was needed was a state with enhanced capacity to lead, manage, and direct our country's economic affairs. This of course entails the modernisation of state systems and processes as well as a highly competent, efficient, and effective bureaucracy.

I argued further that what is most critical is to have a state which can harness big business and other stakeholders within society and make a pact with them to support the state's developmental objectives. The state must be able to galvanise business and other segments of society behind a plan where there is national/societal consensus.

He interjected shortly to remind me that state intervention in an economy produces inefficiencies, and that state intervention creates uncompetitive, unproductive monopolies as we have seen with some of our parastatals. I, in turn, reminded him, that an economy left unchecked by the state produces highly uncompetitive monopolies and oligopolies, as we are currently witnessing in the South African case, where a few big players can control the market both on the supply and demand side, to the exclusion of small businesses and new entrants, with the consequence of stifling innovation and growth that is beneficial to all.

I argued that our focus should be mainly on enhancing the capacity of the state to align big business with a national developmental agenda. Our concern should not just be growth, but also economic and social transformation that will bring about structural and systemic changes that produce broader societal development and improvement of people's lives.

We should rather be focused on the transformation of the institutions and sectors of society so that we produce inclusive and equitable growth, something that the state as an arbiter is best placed to do. I concluded by highlighting the fact that this is what the current government of the day has been endeavouring to do (despite its many critics) and that as a government of revolutionary democrats and not just liberal democrats, the aim has always been to transform the lives of those at the bottom of society and give them a shot at a better life, something which business left to itself is incapable of advancing. I reminded him of the famous words of one of Africa's finest sons, Dr Kwame Nkrumah, when he said, "Seek ye first the political kingdom and all else shall be added unto you". It is this "all else", that government is trying to see added to the people I stated, since political power has already been attained.

We decided to halt the conversation right there and continue it another day, as we had the small matter of a few pints of Guinness to consume and a game of rugby featuring our favourite team, the Blue Bulls to enjoy. On that very sociable note, I decided to acquiesce.

Budget Speech And Implications On The Fight Against Inequality In South Africa

Finance Minister Tito Mboweni's budget speech has come and gone, with the usual varied responses that come with such a crucial annual event on the nation's calendar.

Much has been said about whether the measures introduced by the Treasury will be sufficient to appease global ratings agencies, to avoid another ratings downgrade. My only question here would be whether that should be the uppermost question on our minds, given the multiplicity of problems that we are faced with as a country, but perhaps that question could be an indication of ignorance on my part, so not worth entertaining.

Of course, we must cut expenditure and show fiscal discipline given the problem we are faced with of growing fiscal debt, but from the budget speech one is left with a simple question: how does SA contain spending whilst boosting growth? A former colleague of mine, who deals with matters economic within the Gauteng provincial government and is the quintessential bureaucrat, in discussing the budget speech with me, used a proper bureaucratic phrase when he said that we need to focus on "constraint optimisation" to turn things around.

Apart from the one opposition party, which described the budget as "neo-liberal" (labelling is a favourite South African past-time when we don't have cogent arguments to put forward), the budget seemed to receive a positive response, with most analysts shocked by the tax relief given to South Africans, with personal income tax brackets adjusted above the inflation rate, no VAT increase despite the wild pre-budget speculation, South African corporate tax remaining unchanged at 28%, which is crucial because the tax rates in other countries have fallen, meaning that South Africa has become relatively less competitive as an investment destination.

There is an attempt to broaden the South African tax base and reduce tax rates to promote economic growth, however, the challenge remains that within all this, cutting expenditure has consequences for economic growth. Since 1994 South Africa's fiscal instruments and tax system have been mostly progressive, with South Africa's wealthiest individuals, who earn 63.7% of their income, paying 86.9% of total personal income, according to a 2015 paper on Progressive taxation, Government spending and Inequality in South Africa by: Ingrid Woolard, Rebecca Metz and

Mashekwa Maboshe from the University of Cape Town, Nora Lustig from Tulane University and Gabriela Inchauste and Catriona Purfield from the World Bank.

The very same paper referenced above, states that *"Through progressive taxation and pro-poor social spending, the SA fiscal system reduces income inequality significantly. The extent of this reduction is larger than in twelve comparable middle-income countries measured similarly. Nevertheless, 'final' income (i.e. income after major taxes, government transfers, and spending) remains more unequal than in comparator countries. While the fiscal system has an important role to play in reducing inequality, interventions to improve the distribution of wages, salaries, and capital income are needed."*

So, we are faced with a situation where we celebrate the unexpected tax relief but must cut spending whilst stimulating growth and must implement measures to improve the distribution of wages and salaries in society to address income inequality, whilst looking to cut the public sector wage bill (which must be cut by the way. I support that, in case anyone was wondering whether I would be conflicted on this issue as a civil servant).

So, what does all this mean for the struggle against inequality in South Africa? A 2015 World Bank Study, titled, The Distributional Impact of Fiscal Policy in South Africa, found that, since 1994, *"in large part progress towards greater income equality has proven elusive because of the enduring legacy of the apartheid system. This is true in spite of the fact that South Africa's government has tried to attack the inequality inertia at its roots on several fronts, including most prominently through taxation and social spending."*

I can already hear the commentariat on this platform, in their parochial subjectivity saying, "There goes this dumb, corrupt ANC cadre again, blaming apartheid for everything", but my defence in this case is that I am quoting a World Bank report (which is about as "neoliberal" as it gets as some ideologues are wont to remind us), not my thoughts and preferences. So, despite a progressive fiscal and taxation regime post-1994, we have not dismantled the apartheid legacy, hence we continue to struggle with inequality within our country. How do we dismantle that legacy? Well, that is the question that informs our politics at present and is the subject of much debate within the public space.

What is evident from the two papers I have quoted in this article is that South Africa's fiscal spending and taxation have been very progressive, to the extent that despite growing inequality, our Gini coefficient would have been even higher without these interventions. The World Bank Study finds that, social spending results in sizable increases in the incomes of the poor and that our fiscal policy has achieved appreciable reductions in income inequality and poverty, with these reductions being in fact, the largest in emerging market countries. Despite this, however, levels of inequality and poverty remain high in SA. So, how does one look at the current budget, in light of all these facts?

These are critical things to consider because the growing debt to GDP and debt indicators are an indication of the limited scope that we have as a country, in terms of spending more to achieve greater redistribution. The classical growth/redistribution conundrum still confronts us in these admittedly dark economic times, our "winter of discontent" to quote Shakespeare's Richard III or in more contemporary times, the 1978/79 crisis in Britain. Our hope remains that, in the words of the historical character Mark Antony from the 2005 television series, Rome, *"Winter does not last forever. Spring comes. Snows melt."*

Privatise The Whole Lot, If Needs Be

I was having a conversation with a good mate who happens to be in business, over the past week, and the conversation veered off into him expressing his frustrations with the current state of affairs and its negative impact on business people like him.

My mate happens to be operating in the electricity and power industry, servicing both public and private sector clients within the industry's multi-faceted value chain. We were sitting at a restaurant experiencing load-shedding challenges which meant that some of the items on the menu, could not be ordered, which frustrated both of us, as the unavailable menu options constituted some of the main things that we liked this particular restaurant for.

Anyway, amidst this load-shedding-induced frustration, my mate went on to tell me about a power station that one of the big metros in Gauteng privatised a few years ago, and how this power station was now producing excess capacity which we could be using but are not, because it is Eskom that must facilitate that excess capacity being put on the grid.

We both agreed that this was completely ridiculous and was just one more example of how state-owned monopolies were derailing our growth and development as a nation, due to inefficiencies caused by corruption, ineptitude, indifference, and incompetence amongst other reasons.

We both also agreed that it is really stupid that there are people that are still arguing vociferously against the privatisation of some state-owned entities, despite their inefficiencies crippling the economy, all because of some "stone age" belief in the innate progressiveness of state ownership as a "revolutionary" principle.

In thinking about all this, I was reminded of Joel Netshitenzhe's words when he said, *"Nationalisation in a context of entrenched corruption, weak corporate governance, patronage rather than meritocratic appointments, and disdain for the bottom-line (if our existing state companies are anything to go by), will not deliver improved outcomes with respect to employment, poverty reduction, and reduced inequality."* Substitute the word nationalisation in Netshitenzhe's quote with the phrase state ownership and the same principle still applies.

There is no point in punting state ownership of "strategic assets" within a country, which is supposed to play a positive role in our developmental trajectory, if those state entities are beset by entrenched corruption, weak corporate governance, patronage, and disdain for the bottom-line, which is what we are currently experiencing in most of our state-owned entities.

Most of the people who are proponents of continued ownership of these state-owned entities, despite their obvious current state of shambles, appear to miss or be ignorant of the point that the role of the state should be adjusted to the needs of the national economy, with more or less state ownership being advanced at any given point in time, based on what would be of benefit to the national economy and the nation as a whole.

We need a stable, reliable power supply, which Eskom, for whatever reasons you may be personally comfortable with accepting is unable to give at present, so if guaranteeing that stable, reliable power supply requires that one privatise the whole thing, then so be it. Privatise the whole damn thing if needs be and leave the ideologues to go argue the merits and demerits of such a step in their elite, intellectual corners. The rest of us in South African society just want something that works, not banal ideological struggles that add no value to our lived experiences on a daily basis.

The issue is not whether one is for or against state ownership, but rather to reduce or increase state ownership and involvement in certain areas in ways that will enhance efficiency, enable economic growth, facilitate economic inclusivity, and bring about better living standards for all of us as South Africans.

The debate over state ownership is old and stale and is of no interest to the majority of South Africans, what they want is something that works and is reliable and cost-effective, so that they can focus on improving their own lives and circumstances. If state-owned entities aren't contributing to that, then the most revolutionary and progressive thing to do, if putting the people's interests first is truly the priority, is to sell those state interests off to those who will run them efficiently and optimally to their own benefit through making a profit and that of society through better, more reliable, more cost-effective services.

Of course, the state would still play a role in regulating those sectors of the economy in which these state-owned entities that are sold off are operating, to guarantee and ensure the public good, but even that need not be an antagonistic activity in the context of our developmental aspirations as a people. So, we need to stop this polarising South African phenomenon of tackling both/and issues with an either/or mindset.

So, whilst in agreement with sentiments of increasing or building state capacity to drive development, I don't think that focusing on that precludes us from using private sector capacity to achieve our aims and objectives. In the words of Joel Netshitenzhe once again, *"In speaking of a developmental state, we are shifting away from an exaggerated state-centredness to stressing partnerships, from structure to relationships, and from blueprint planning to process. In the context of our particular transition, this approach to the state also underlines why we need to be thinking about the transformation/restructuring of the state and state assets..."*

The point with all of this is that it's not about holding on to dogmatic, outdated ideological stances, but about finding out what would work best in each instance and then implementing it. So, if at a certain period (like the present), we need to shed off certain state assets to facilitate inclusive growth and development, then so be it. What matters most, is what would be of most benefit to South Africa and South Africans, or as so well-articulated in the African National Congress' 1969 Morogoro conference strategy and tactics document, the point is to ensure in every decision taken, that *"the basic resources of our country are at the disposal of the people as a whole and not manipulated by sectors or individuals be they White or Black."*

Ideology And Ideologues Are Holding Us Back

The crippling SAA strike this week, with the already struggling airline losing tens of millions daily as a result, reminded me once again of the dangers of ideology and how we as a country are being held back by the narrow convictions of ideologues who continue to dominate the public space.

The South African government has pumped billions into supposedly saving a struggling airline that should have been sold off years ago, but because we live in a country where some have posited state ownership as the supreme principle behind our developmental aspirations, this has tragically not happened, and we keep wasting taxpayers' money on an entity that has been on life support for too long.

The same thing could be said about Eskom, where National Treasury released a discussion document a couple of months ago on how to turn the SA economy around, and one of the suggestions was that selling off Eskom's coal power stations could help the embattled state-owned entity resolve its crippling debt-burden, but once again the ideologues who place a high premium on state ownership above all other realities shouted the loudest and won the day.

Now I know that some people are still stuck in a 20th century, Cold War mindset and accuse anyone who is a member of the ANC of being a Marxist, but I consider myself a pragmatic fellow who is not tied into any "isms" and who is more concerned with what would work for the country as opposed to dogmatically advancing a certain ideological perspective. I often joke with some of my mates that the only Marxism I subscribe to, if one were to try and box me, would be that of Groucho Marx, as in I have this innate ability to find humour in any situation, no matter how serious it may be.

In thinking of all this in frustration at how ideology and ideologues are holding us back, I was reminded of a 1992 document by the ANC aptly titled, **Ready to Govern**. In discussing the highly contested matter of state ownership, the document states the following, *"state ownership is not posited as the in-principle alternative to all private monopolies: rather, this would be informed by the impact such ownership would have on the ability of the economy to address poverty and inequality and to encourage* *growth and competitiveness. Secondly, the developmental state should be responsible for enterprises that provide public goods such as infrastructure and basic services. Thirdly, the private sector, including monopoly capital, is treated not as an enemy, but as a potential partner-and yet one that needs to be regulated. Lastly, a balance of evidence would inform such decisions to either increase or reduce the public sector while protecting consumers and workers."*

It is quite self-evident that keeping limping parastatals such as Eskom and SAA under state ownership because of some silly ideological inclinations does nothing to help the fight against poverty and inequality, it does nothing to encourage the growth and competitiveness of our economy, it does nothing to protect workers and consumers and on the objective *"balance of evidence"*, in a society of reasonable people, it wouldn't be such a big deal if these where sold off to private hands where they could be run and managed more efficiently to the greater public good. Of course, these entities would still be regulated to ensure they serve the public good even in private hands, but that wouldn't necessarily prevent them from pursuing profit whilst still doing so, as some leftist ideologues would not want them to.

So, our problem is that we are held to ransom by ideologues, with their religious devotion to their ideologies, even at the expense of the greater public good. It reminds one of the words of the author J. Adam Snyder, when he said, *"An ideologue is one who places agenda above truth."* In South Africa, the ideological agenda seems to be the given pre-eminence, even if it's clearly setting us back.

Witness how, even the main opposition party has almost totally collapsed itself in the past couple of months, all because some within it want to restore it to *its "classical liberal"* posture. So, on all sides of the political spectrum, it would appear that we are being held to ransom as a country by ideologues with their *"righteous convictions"* about their parochial beliefs and value systems. All of this ignores the simple fact that we live in a complex world, which requires nuanced responses that address objective realities as opposed to perceived ones. As US historian Morris Berman once said, *"An idea is something that you have, an ideology is something that has you."* People who are possessed by their ideological convictions are some of the biggest enemies of progress in this country.

Going back to the contested issue of state ownership of entities that are clearly draining the public purse and not contributing positively towards our developmental agenda, one has to go back to the principles referred to earlier in the ANC's 1992 **Ready to Govern** document, and with that conclude that there is nothing innately progressive or revolutionary about state ownership just like there would be nothing innately counter-revolutionary about privatisation of these state-owned assets. What matters most, in deciding between the two options at any given time, are the objective conditions that we are confronted with as well as the possibilities identified in response to those objective conditions. Blind loyalty to ideology and dogma won't take us anywhere as a country.

When Franklin D. Roosevelt, for example, decided to implement his New Deal in America in the 1930s, the critical consideration there wasn't ideological, but what would work best to resuscitate the American economy post the Great Depression. They weren't interested in resolving ideological debates about the supposed supremacy of the classical economics school over other economic ideologies, hence the New Deal focussed on reforming the US financial sector and rolling out big public works projects to help the US economy recover. Ideology then, as now, does nothing to help when economic turnaround is needed. Would that we would understand this in contemporary South Africa.

Happy Days Are Here Again

Listening to President Matamela Cyril Ramaphosa announcing his new team of special investment envoys with a plan to raise around $100 billion over the next five years by travelling the globe and selling the South African story of openness and opportunity to potential investors reminded one of the lyrics to American Jazz Age (an era wonderfully captured in F. Scott Fitzgerald's timeless novel, The Great Gatsby) singer Annette Hanshaw's song Happy Days are Here Again, "Happy days are here again, The skies above are clear again, Let us sing a song of cheer again, Happy days are here again, Altogether shout it now, There's no one who can doubt it now, So let's tell the world about it now, Happy days are here again…"

President Ramaphosa's "New Dawn" is upon us, and we have entered into an "age of opportunity" as a nation. The doom and gloom of the Zuma years appear to be aeons of years behind us. Such nebulous, subjective concepts as business confidence, consumer confidence and political risk seem to suddenly be working in our favour, totally contrary to what we witnessed in the previous decade under the leadership of President Zuma.

There is renewed positivity and hype around South Africa and the South African story, with a leading global investment bank having recently tipped South Africa to be the leading "emerging market story (economically) of 2018." The economy is tipped to grow at a higher rate than had previously been anticipated; the President himself declared this to be the "year of the job" as the country continues to fight to overcome unacceptably high levels of unemployment and inequality. So, this is the message that our new special investment envoys will be conveying as they traverse the globe and various corners of South Africa in pursuit of the highly sought-after foreign and domestic direct investment. The wonderful part of the story is also that big business appears to be on board and we are seemingly well on course to turning our economic fortunes around and overcoming the much-talked-about investment strike by the private sector.

Anyone who loves this country and wants us to overcome all our demons and become the South Africa of "opportunity and plenty" would of course celebrate all this and put their hands on deck to contribute positively to this much-needed turnaround. But alas, what if big business itself is part of the problem with the South

African economic story, as it stands today before this much-desired turnaround?

A 2016 University of Johannesburg Centre for Competition, Regulation and Economic Development (CCRED) study titled, **An Agenda for Opening up the South African Economy: Lessons from Studies of Barriers to Entry** by Professor Simon Roberts tells us that a large part of the problem with the South African economy is that across various sectors it is dominated by a monopoly of a few small firms which control entire value chains and have market power which enables them to control the terms of trade.

This uncompetitive behaviour by these few large firms has the net effect of preventing the entry and growth of small businesses in the South African market. This is a serious impediment to inclusive economic growth because it is small businesses that provide the innovation and impetus that grow an economy and create much-needed jobs. It stifles investment, innovation and initiative within the economy because the few big players can keep new entrants and other small businesses from growing to protect their market share and dominant positions. Whilst this may be of huge benefit to the shareholders and owners of these few big corporates, it works against the developmental objectives of the country and proves once again as the report highlights that markets are innately imperfect and incapable of self-correcting, contrary to what those who subscribe to the classical school of economics would have us believe.

So, there is a point at which big business in its search for profits (often super profits owing to their dominant market position) ends up also scuppering the growth and job-creating potential of our economy. The solution of course is to open up the South African market and make it more competitive, meaning that these big monopolies must be broken up to allow small businesses and entrepreneurs to flourish.

Our Competition Commission must have more teeth, not just to fine big players for uncompetitive behaviour, but also to break them up to create more inclusive, equitable growth. We need to create an economy where ease of entry is sacrosanct and big business is enticed (or forced) to open up value chains so that we can win the battle against unemployment and inequality and truly enter into this "New Dawn" that President Ramaphosa is leading us towards. After all, as the UJ CCRED report reminds us, the NDP states that one of the main problems with the phenomenon of highly concentrated industries that have limited competition is that they produce little (if any) efficiency gains within an economy.

In the end, we should have a both-and (as opposed to either-or) approach to this issue. We need big business to invest more in our economy and initiatives such as the government's InvestSA one-stop-shop and the appointment of special investment envoys should be celebrated in this regard, but the other big favour that patriotic South African corporates can do for us, is to open up the value chain, open up markets and give or create opportunities for small players to come in so that we can indeed grow the economy, create jobs, and address the income and asset inequality that stubbornly remains an albatross around our necks as a nation.

Dr Richard Maponya and the Township Economy

Upon hearing of the death of black business legend Dr Richard Maponya this week, I was reminded of those timeless, poignant words from Thomas Babington Macaulay's Lays of Ancient Rome, *"Then out spake brave Horatius, The Captain of the Gate: To every man upon this earth, death cometh soon or late, and how can man die better, than facing fearful odds, for the ashes of his fathers, and the temples of his gods."*

Dr Richard Maponya was a guru, a father of the township economy who fought against immeasurable odds that apartheid placed against black business at the time and became for the rest of us a shining example of what could be achieved with a bit of entrepreneurial initiative, drive, ambition, innovation, and singlemindedness. Having built a successful business empire emanating from Soweto, Dr Maponya's life was the embodiment of the words of distinguished journalist, editor and media personality Aggrey Klaaste when he said, *"Soweto is a metaphor for Black lives in South Africa."*

When reflecting on the life of Dr Maponya, we must of necessity reflect on the struggles of black business to find expression within the mainstream economy of South Africa and ask ourselves whether we are doing enough to inculcate a culture of entrepreneurship in our townships as a means towards facilitating economic and spatial transformation, growing our economy more equitably and sustainably and of course creating much-needed jobs.

I was reminded of the argument advanced by renowned scenario planner Clem Sunter, when he opined that government should not be setting itself job creation targets for the economy per se, but rather should be focusing on promoting, supporting, and facilitating the growth of sustainable SMMEs, as in the long run, these sustainable SMMEs are the ones that will create the jobs that are needed in the economy to deal with unemployment and poverty. It is a question of focus and prioritisation, more than anything, which is well captured in the words of Dr Maponya himself, when he was talking about the importance of entrepreneurs, *"as they grow their businesses, they address poverty as well. Believe you me, with more people creating job opportunities-this country could turn around overnight and the kind of poverty we see will be a thing of the past. I'm hoping I can see this happening in my lifetime."*

Dr Maponya passed away without seeing this vision come to pass, but we owe it to his rich legacy to ensure that we fight to bring it to fruition. We must support and promote entrepreneurship within the townships in honour of his rich legacy and vision. We must aggressively advocate for the development of black businesses, building viable, sustainable, competitive, innovative township enterprises and black-owned and managed entities. We must convert our townships from labour reserves and consumption centres into hubs of productive economic activity and entrepreneurial nous that produce enterprises and entities that can capture greater swathes of the value chain within various sectors of our economy.

This requires interventions that will promote the growth and development of manufacturing and the productive capacity of township businesses. This is why the Gauteng provincial government, has dedicated itself to investing in catalytic economic infrastructure that will build and develop manufacturing capacity in the townships, through township industrial hubs and agri-hubs that have the potential to boost exports into the rest of Africa and other parts of the world.

Another novel initiative that is in line with the ideals of Dr Maponya as the quintessential township entrepreneur, is efforts by the Gauteng provincial government, working in conjunction with municipalities, to release government-owned land under its Rapid Land Release programme for commercial activities in the townships as well as the work on a Township Development Act that will help address some of the regulatory, legislative, and administrative bottlenecks that prevent township businesses from flourishing.

Efforts have also been made to use private and public sector procurement spending to invest in the growth and development of township enterprises, with provincial government spending on township enterprises growing from R600 million per annum at the beginning of the fifth term of office in 2014 to roughly R22 billion by the end of that term in 2019. These are all significant steps that show progress, but of course much more still needs to be done to ensure that township enterprises don't just participate in state procurement as rent-seeking middlemen, but rather as value-adding producers. Also, there is a great need for private sector supplier development and enterprise development initiatives to prioritise the development and support of township enterprises to open new markets for them as well as ensure their participation within sectoral value chains in the economy.

Given that Dr Maponya was the brains behind the iconic Maponya Mall in Soweto, one of the critical interventions that needs to be looked into, is the impact of retail developments in the townships on local SMME development as well as on the productive capacity of the township economy as well as the money flow (does money flow into the township and circulate to stimulate other economic activities as a result of these retail developments in the townships, or does money just merely flow out of the townships through consumption from these developments?)

Dr Maponya was a fervent believer in investing in and developing the capacity of township enterprises and black businesses as a means towards building a better, more inclusive, prosperous and equitable South Africa and in honouring his legacy, this is a struggle that we must look to intensify. Ever the innovator and entrepreneur, at the age of 94 he launched a poultry farm, trying to get small farmers in Winterveldt in Tshwane as one example, to use the land they have access to optimally, as part of his minor contribution to agricultural reform. Upon receiving a lifetime achievement award at the inaugural Township Entrepreneur Awards launched by the Gauteng provincial government in 2016, Dr Maponya said the following words in his acceptance speech, which are an embodiment of his profound belief in the support and development of black business as one of the key pillars in tackling our socio-economic problems as a country, *"we have the power, we have the numbers, we can do it. The future is in our hands. If Black people can support one another like we see other racial groups do, we will definitely control the purse strings of this country."*

No Need for a State Bank

At the recent ANC National Policy Conference, I found myself sitting next to a senior ANC leader at plenary on the last day and we ended up having a very intense and informative discussion about economic policy issues, among which was the idea of forming a state bank, which this senior ANC leader was in support of.

I argued that the ANC does not need to advocate for a state bank in order to advance its economic transformation objectives, because firstly if we look at the current status of our State Owned Entities (SOEs) which are supposed to be primary drivers of development within the context of our aspirant developmental state, neither we as honest, sincere, patriotic ANC members who put South Africa first nor the rest of society has any objective reason for believing that the ANC-led government can run a state bank efficiently and effectively in order to advance its socio-economic transformation agenda.

I know this is radical, mind-boggling stuff for those out there who believe that people who are in the ANC can never be objective, but one can't ignore the glaringly obvious and damning facts before us, as relates to the state of our SOEs. My second point, which may be more palatable to some within the organisation than my first one, was that one does not need a state bank to try and transform the economy and solve the problem of black exclusion from access to capital and other financial services sector products that would enable black people to play a more significant role within the mainstream economy, and a good example of this is seen in how the Afrikaaner people built their own private financial services sector institutions, including banks, in order to resolve the same problem, which they were faced with in the 1930s and 1940s.

A point from the ANC's 1992 Ready to Govern document bears referencing in this regard, "State ownership is not posited as the in-principle alternative to all private monopolies: rather, this would be informed by the impact such ownership would have on the ability of the economy to address poverty and inequality and to encourage growth and competitiveness. Secondly, the developmental state should be responsible for enterprises that provide public goods such as infrastructure and basic services. Thirdly, the private sector, including monopoly capital, is treated not as an enemy, but as a potential partner – and yet one that needs to be regulated. Lastly, the balance of evidence would inform decisions to either increase or reduce the public sector while protecting consumers and workers." There is nothing innately progressive about state ownership per se, just like there is nothing innately counter-revolutionary about private ownership. What is important at every juncture is to look at state capacity to drive development, investment and the economy at large as well as the ability of the state to direct and channel the private sector to national development aims and objectives.

In the 1930s, out of a realisation that they would never achieve their objective of self-determination without actually attaining economic power, Die Volk convened an economic Volkskongress in Kimberly to come up with workable solutions to their problem of economic marginalisation. This was the brain child of the Afrikaner Broederbond (I am still of the persuasion that the ANC itself needs a Broederbond of sorts behind it if it is ever to truly renew itself, along the Leninist "better fewer but better" principle ironically enough, but that is a discussion for another day and another opinion piece from me perhaps), who appreciated the simple fact that economic power was a necessary pre-condition for Afrikaner self-determination and as such the latter would not be attainable without the former.

Out of this Volkskongress was birthed the idea of building financial institutions that would bridge the gap of access to funding for Afrikaner peoples, as established financial institutions at the time were not playing ball when it came to giving ordinary Afrikaners access to capital and funding for various economic activities that are part of developing yourself as a people group.

One of the many institutions that were formed as part of this resolve, was a bank which became a colossal institution that advanced Afrikaner developmental interests, Volkskas Bank, a bank that was formed with the aid and assistance of the government, through the Ministry of Finance. It grew to become one of the four largest banks in South Africa under the National Party government and was one of the three biggest Afrikaner monopolies in the country at the time, even investing in other industries beyond banking to the point that almost half of its profits came from its industrial endeavours at a point in the 1980s. So, even the quest for black industrialists is doomed to fail, if we do not address this particular issue of transforming the financial services sector by promoting and supporting the development of black institutions within this critical economic sector, which drives all other economic activity in fact.

Volkskas was an Afrikaaner Bank, an institution (amongst banks and financial institutions that Afrikaaners built during the time) that was brought about as a result of concerted, deliberate efforts by Afrikaners to transform the economy in their favour using state power so as to become a powerful force economically.

What began as a humble cooperative bank grew into a powerful commercial banking and industrial conglomerate, with the turning point coming in the late 1940s when the National Party came to power. Volkskas was formed specifically to address the economic impoverishment of Afrikaaners (along with other Afrikaner businesses that grew to become conglomerates and today are even competing at a multi-national level).

These were private institutions that were supported by the state, through the National Party government (with the Broederbond running the strings in the background), but none of them lost their developmental thrust and impact on the Afrikaner people. With the coming of the National party to power in 1948, state power was used to channel funds to Afrikaner businesses such as Volkskas.

The Broederbond were at the forefront of all this and these were the finest and sharpest amongst the Afrikaner community, who were very patriotic when it came to the advancement of Afrikaner interests. The Afrikaners basically implemented cadre deployment effectively, deploying the best amongst themselves to take over the state and other aspects of South African society in order to advance Afrikaner interests and ensure that they brought about Afrikaner economic emancipation and self-determination, through channelling resources and funds to Afrikaner business entities that were patriotic insofar as it came to Afrikaner people.

Therefore, instead of dogmatically advancing for a state bank, perhaps we should be looking at developing black-owned, black-run banks and financial services businesses that will contribute to our developmental aspirations. Patriotic black capital within the financial services sector and other sectors of the economy is what we should be focussing on producing, using state power and resources, just like the National Party did, in order to bring that about. Even in a highly developed capitalist state such as the United States of America, capital is highly patriotic and never goes against the aims and objectives of the nation-state.

China, which is celebrated for having developed "socialism with Chinese characteristics"(it is just another form of state capitalism in my view, but I will let you decide on that one) has developed a whole range of business enterprises, many of them privately owned and run, which are subject to the developmental aims and objectives of the state and where they veer off, the state is capacitated enough to be able to discipline them and bring them back into line with national development aspirations, as we have seen Xi Jinping doing, very successfully so in fact, in the past couple of years.

I am reminded of a conversation I had over a couple of pints with a mate of mine from my varsity days who is now a leader in the financial services sector, not too long ago. He said to me, "Mugsy, you okes have over R2 trillion in government spend per annum in order to drive economic transformation, so why do you okes often complain as if you don't have the capacity to do so? With that kind of spend, you okes can even direct private sector investment towards the areas that you deem critical for national development, but it seems as if there is no political will to do so. Why does the ANC act like a powerless opposition party when it has so much leverage as a party that has been in government for so long?" To highlight his point even further, total consolidated government spending will amount to R6.62 trillion over the next three years.

Government must not only use its annual spend, but also vehicles such as the Public Investment Corporation and the Eskom Pension and Provident Fund as pertinent examples, to drive economic transformation and build black banks and financial services institutions in order to bring about economic transformation and development, as opposed to taking workers' money and investing it in ventures such as Bounty Brands, which have no developmental thrust and transformative impact, but rather contribute to capital flight and the loss of the money of workers. The Unemployment Insurance Fund, whose money and investments are managed by the Public Investment Corporation, recently lost R1.8 billion in public money by indirectly investing in Bounty Brands. This is money that belongs to South African workers, which is a crucial safety net for those workers who become unemployed.

Government should have facilitated the growth and development of banks such as VBS and Ithala into those kinds of transformative, developmental entities like Volkskas was, but instead, the reverse is happening and we are actually seeing these entities being collapsed and destroyed. Government should have been able to facilitate the mobilising of money from stokvels and burial societies, to develop those kinds of patriotic, developmental black-owned entities.

The ANC-led government has to be decisive, unapologetic and intentional about building black banks, black financial services institutions, like the National Party did with the likes of Volkskas Bank, Sanlam etc. This must be implemented whilst heeding the words of Frantz Fanon in his book, The Wretched of the Earth, "The national middle class which takes over power at the end of the colonial regime is an under-developed middle class. It has practically no economic power, and in any case, it is in no way commensurate with the bourgeoisie of the mother country which it hopes to replace. In its wilful narcissism, the national middle class is easily convinced that it can advantageously replace the middle class of the mother country.

But that same independence which literally drives it into a comer will give rise within its ranks to catastrophic reactions and will oblige it to send out frenzied appeals for help to the former mother country. The university and merchant classes which make up the most enlightened section of the new state are in fact characterized by the smallness of their number, their being concentrated in the capital, and the type of activities in which they are engaged: business, agriculture and the liberal professions.

Neither financiers nor industrial magnates are to be found within this national middle class. The national bourgeoisie of under-developed countries is not engaged in production, nor in invention, nor building, nor labour; it is completely canalized into activities of the intermediary type. Its innermost vocation seems to be to keep in the running and to be part of the racket. The psychology of the national bourgeoisie is that of the businessman, not that of a captain of industry; and it is only too true that the greed of the settlers and the system of embargoes set up by colonialism has hardly left them any other choice.

Under the colonial system, a middle class which accumulates capital is an impossible phenomenon. Now, precisely, it would seem that the historical vocation of an authentic national middle class in an under-developed country is to repudiate its own nature in so far as it is bourgeois, that is to say in so far as it is the tool of capitalism, and to make itself the willing slave of that revolutionary capital which is the people.

In an under-developed country an authentic national middle class ought to consider as its bounden duty to betray the calling fate has marked out for it, and to put itself to school with the people: in other words to put at the people's disposal the intellectual and technical capital that it has snatched when going through the colonial universities."

2

TRANSFORM OR PERISH

Transformation is an Existential Necessity

I was reading James Myburgh's interesting piece on transformation supposedly killing South Africa, https://www.politicsweb.co.za/opinion/transformation-is-killing-south-africa and found myself reflecting on how far we are from our nation-building objectives as a people because I realised that the opinion being expressed by James in this piece represents the views of many South Africans who feel excluded from this South Africa that we are currently building, hence arguments about whether white South Africans should stay or go currently enjoy much traction amongst the various sections of our society, as outlined by a couple of articles written within this forum over the past couple of weeks or so.

To hammer this point home further, a mate of mine from my varsity days who is a highly intelligent chap, a qualified professional with experience at a senior level within multi-national corporations and who has also lived abroad and hence has had much exposure (he's not parochial) had this to say on social media in a post over the past week, *"the Mandela project didn't work. It was superficial and did not address the hard truths. Stay or go, it really doesn't matter unless we deal with the underlying issues. The first thing being structural, race-based inequality."*

Different groupings within the very same society showing diverse perspectives on a topical issue, nothing new there, apart from the fact that the issue that these views are being expressed about will determine whether South Africa becomes or does not become what former President Thabo Mbeki spoke about in a Nelson Mandela memorial lecture at Wits in 2006, *"the great masses of our country every day pray that the new South Africa that is being born will be a good, a moral, a humane, and a caring South Africa, which, as it matures, will progressively guarantee the happiness of all its citizens."* Idealistic stuff right, but are we anywhere near achieving such high existential ideals as a people, and if not why?

Well, to quote former President Mbeki again, in his 1978 speech, The Historical Injustice, *"All societies therefore necessarily bear the imprint, the birthmarks of their own past. Whether to a greater or lesser extent must depend on a whole concatenation of factors, both internal and external to each particular society."* We must start by acknowledging the fact that not too long ago, those who held political and economic power considered it appropriate (despite the convenient denialism of many in the current epoch) to instil policies that ensured the marginalisation and subjugation of the black African majority.

This is the history which we come from and that we are trying to break out of, but we will never do so until we acknowledge that this history has a direct bearing on where we find ourselves today and the fact that we have an economy, which is still to a large extent characterised by mostly white males being at the top of the food chain (despite persistent cries of white victimhood in this regard, this remains an empirical fact) and the black, African masses being at the very bottom and still largely excluded from the mainstream.

All of this necessitates a radical change, a shift to reverse the effects of the unjust past on the current prospects of the black majority, and hence the need for transformation. As my mate, former Springbok Luke Watson once stated in a brilliant talk on transformation that he gave at the UCT rugby club hosted by Ubumbo (a rugby club within the UCT internal league), which sadly got reduced to his comment about "puking on the Springbok rugby jersey" (I was there and his passing comment which we all laughed off in a light-hearted manner was taken out of context and completely blown out of proportion, but I digress), transformation is about a change of mindset and attitude before anything else.

This is of course very difficult and as a result, most people are resistant to it, but here's the thing, transformation requires a change of mindset and attitude from both black and white South Africans, as Luke Watson highlighted and without that change of mindset and attitude on both sides, we are not going anywhere as a country and in fact, we'll end up in a rut which seems like quicksand that we can't get out of. So, au contraire, it is not the transformation that is killing South Africa, but rather the refusal to truly embrace genuine transformation that is holding us back from becoming the Rainbow Nation that belongs to all who live in it as the Freedom Charter enjoins.

The point is that the current structure upon which South African society is built (inherited from our divided past) is unsustainable and highly untenable for most South Africans and hence it needs to be uprooted to promote inclusivity and bring about greater cohesion. This requires an internal transformation from all sides, which will have uncomfortable outward ramifications in the interim, but these are the growing pains that we need to embrace if we are ever to achieve the ultimate objective of non-racialism. The steps towards maturing into a non-racial democracy require that hard decisions be taken to change the status quo. We can't wish that away.

The end goal is to transform South Africa into a non-racial country at all levels of human interaction and action and transform gender relations to deal with historic gender inequalities. This inequality was entrenched through policies and of course, it must be reversed through policies as well.

We must of necessity deracialise our economy so that it's more inclusive and this requires policy interventions to reverse past injustices of course, there are those who like Holocaust denialists, want to deny the existence of such past injustices (apartheid like the Holocaust was declared a crime against humanity lest we forget so there are parallels to be drawn here, down to the fact that there were reparations that were paid for the Holocaust, but no such restitution was arranged for the evils of apartheid) and their current impact, who claim we must "just move on", but that's akin to living in a fool's paradise.

So, we may argue against the mechanisms for restitution against past injustices, such as BEE and EE, but then we must find and suggest alternate solutions to do so if we are ever going to move towards a deracialised, integrated, united society that is our ideal. To merely write off transformation as a killer to the nation-building project, without bringing to the table workable mechanisms to make amends for the past with all its current effects is to live in an ahistorical and unrealistic world.

The argument that the African National Congress-led post-94 government is advancing "racial goals" is ahistorical and unrealistic because it doesn't consider the fact that the policies that this government has set in place, have been aimed at reversing the effects of the past to move towards non-racialism. You would be hard-pressed to find a greater champion for non-racialism than the African National Congress.

It is quite interesting that even the main opposition is struggling with this transformation issue, hence the internal squabbles that we are currently witnessing that have led to exposes on its current leader which some claim are coming from "white liberals" who want to take their party back. So, whoever you are and wherever you are in South African society, you have to reckon with the burden of transformation, like it or not.

Let me also add that a truly transformed, non-racial South Africa will embrace and encourage heterogeneity, as opposed to suppressing it. So, for example, in such a society, we would celebrate and not criticise the opening of a new Afrikaans university, as it would be seen as contributing towards the promotion and development of a language and culture which forms part of our unique DNA as a people and would hopefully encourage other indigenous language groups to do the same, under the guise of nation-building.

So, on the contrary, the African National Congress-led government does not and has never had a racial agenda as falsely alleged by those who critique its transformation policies, but rather it is because of its aim of building a non-racial society that it must pursue transformation as an existential imperative.

The ANC-led government's motivation and motive for seeking to transform South African society, is encapsulated in these words uttered by former President Thabo Mbeki in a speech I referred to earlier, way back in 1978, *"Yet this is what a free South Africa will be like. For as the masses themselves long discovered, the antithesis to White supremacy, exclusiveness and arrogance is not a Black version of the same practice.*

In the physical world, Black might indeed be the opposite of White. But in the world of social systems, social theory and practice have as much to do with skin pigmentation as has the birth of children with the stork. To connect the two is to invent a fable with the conscious or unconscious purpose of hiding reality.

The act of negating the theory and practice of White apartheid racism, the revolutionary position, is exactly to take the issue of colour, race, national and sex differentiation out of the sphere of rational human thinking and behaviour, and thereby expose all colour, race, nation and sex prejudice as irrational." Other parties might be advancing a multi-racial or anti-racism agenda, but all of these are completely different to non-racialism, which is the ANC-led government's end goal, with transformation as a means towards that end goal.

Transformation Of The Financial Services Sector: An Objective Necessity

As the motive forces of the National Democratic Revolution (NDR) become increasingly impatient with the rate and pace of change in South African society, one of the main criticisms has been that the

ANC-led government has lacked the boldness, decisiveness and political will to radically transform the economy towards greater inclusivity and more equitable outcomes, that favour the black majority in general and Africans in particular.

The ANC-led government is often criticised for not having been aggressive enough in using the levers of state power to ensure that there is a fundamental, systemic transformation of the South African economy so that it loses its apartheid-era racial and gender composition of ownership, control, and management of our economy.

At the 1969 Morogoro Conference, oft-quoted and referenced, the ANC affirmed in its strategy and tactics document that, *"In our country, it is inconceivable for liberation to have meaning without a return of the wealth of the land to the people as a whole. To allow the existing economic forces to retain their interests intact is to feed the root of racial supremacy and does not represent even the shadow of liberation. Our drive towards national emancipation is therefore in a very real way bound up with economic emancipation. Our people are deprived of their due in the country's wealth; their skills have been suppressed and poverty and starvation have been their life experience. The correction of these centuries-old economic injustices lies at the very core of our national aspirations."*

Whilst admitting to the fact that much progress has been made in transforming the economy, one would not be completely out of touch with reality if one made the observation that within the current dispensation, there is a need for accelerated implementation of long-standing ANC policies in order to ensure that we bring about economic transformation, growing the economy in an inclusive, equitable, job creating manner so that the people do indeed share in the wealth of the country and achieve their desired aspirations of a better life.

We must ensure that we use state power in order to disrupt the status quo so as to materially better the lives of the people and deliver on their hopes and aspirations. We have to be more aggressive about ensuring that we are advancing in our quest for a more just and equitable society.

We have to be bolder, more decisive, and unapologetic about pursuing historical redress, the correction of past injustices and imbalances which still have a material effect on our people's potential or on opportunities for social and economic advancement and about bringing about redistribution; income, wealth, and asset redistribution in order to reduce inequality.

In seeking to advance this more radical agenda, we must of course always be cognisant of the following critical facts, that also stem from the ANC's 1969 strategy and tactics document at Morogoro:

- A revolutionary policy is one which holds out the quickest and most fundamental transformation of power from one class to another.
- Such radical changes are not brought about by imaginary forces but by those whose outlook and readiness to act are influenced by historically determined factors.
- The art of revolutionary leadership consists in providing leadership to the masses and not just its most advanced elements, it consists of setting a pace which accords with objective conditions and real possibilities at hand.
- A revolutionary-sounding phrase does not always reflect revolutionary policy and revolutionary policy is not always the springboard for revolutionary advance.
- Often what appears to be militant, and revolutionary can turn out to be counter-revolutionary.

So, in looking to fast-track the transformation of our economy, we should shy away from populist rhetoric and cheap sloganeering which have no material impact on the lives of ordinary South Africans but instead are informed by predatory instincts. We must however be bold, aggressive, and unapologetic about economic transformation, using the state as a primary driver of our progressive agenda. The time for equivocation and a softly, softly approach has long passed. This is fundamental to the achievement of our historical goals and objectives as a people's movement.

We must be geared towards forming partnerships within society that will help advance our revolutionary objectives. In all that we do, we must ensure that our approach will have the following effect and impact: increase the black share of wealth and income, increase employment and investment within the economy, decrease inequality and bring inclusive growth, enable us to increase the skills base within society (e.g. provide access to education, skills development etc.) so that we can give better opportunities to the people. The broader agenda is that we must be able to transform our economy so that the masses of the people can achieve an improved quality of life.

Given the phenomenon of the increased financialisation of the economy and economic activity, one of the strategic areas of focus in transforming the South African economy, is the financial services sector and one of the most crucial vehicles that we possess as a party that is in government, that we have not utilised optimally, is the Public Investment Corporation (PIC), which has roughly R3 trillion in assets under management on behalf of the working class, which must be used to advance working-class interests in transforming the economy.

Less than 10% of the R9 trillion of assets within the financial services sector (roughly R3 trillion under the PIC) in South Africa, are deployed to black asset managers, so there is obviously a need for a more aggressive transformation drive within the sector, using the PIC as a primary driver to ensure that the children of the working class, who become the black asset managers and aspirant players within the financial services sector, become significant players when it comes to being on the table of asset allocation.

Our current legislation requires trustees to use asset consultants and so, we may be perpetuating the problem through our own laws. Trustees may want to deploy capital to black fund managers, but the law says they have to rely on asset consultants and asset consultants are mainly white, so this is an area that we need to zoom in on in pursuit of the transformation of the financial services sector.

The PIC must primarily use black asset consultants. The asset consultants are the gate keepers that determine where pension fund money goes. There is no reason why black asset managers, run by children of the working class, should not be entrusted with managing the funds of the working class. The black asset consultants should have a bias towards black asset managers, to the extent that black asset managers perform (and there is no evidence that indicates a lack of capacity and underperformance of black asset managers at present). There must be a mandate from government, unapologetically so, to ensure that this becomes the case.

What is extremely important is that this is not only about black participation in capital allocation but investments in growing black-owned asset classes in the broader economy. We do not want black asset managers to still be allocating liquidity ostensibly in portfolios where black ownership does not exist. The PICs mandate must come with conditionalities that enforce significant transformation and black ownership requirements, in the investment portfolios, whether listed or unlisted. This can be encouraged also through performance fees, factoring revenue expense ratios etc.

This is important so that we not only transform the asset management industry and financial services sector but also regulate the nature and texture of asset classes where liquidity is channelled by black or white asset managers, so as to reach and transform the broader economy.

There are three critical focus areas that can enable us to practically implement our transformation agenda within the financial services sector:

- The PIC must drastically increase allocation mandates to black asset managers and sponsor further training for new entrants so that the pool keeps growing. The PIC must foster partnerships with established white asset managers

65

to work with upcoming black firms.

- We must regulate investment portfolios to reflect our broader strategic objectives to deracialise the economy. Furthermore, we must streamline Financial Sector Conduct Authority (FSCA) regulatory and compliance to be consistent with these requirements.

- Liquidity to be channelled to bolstering black ownership, transformation, and asset classes with strong ESG (environmental, social and governance) undertones.

Conquest Is The Way Forward

Out of my fascination with the legend that is Shaka Zulu, I recently picked up a book by the Oxford-educated thinker and business leader, Professor Phinda Madi, titled, Leadership Lessons from Emperor Shaka Zulu. The book itself is about the story of a young consultant operating within the corporate environment in the South who is working in a company that is encountering serious problems due to leadership failures/flaws (sounds very familiar doesn't it?)

Whilst undergoing stress related to his work environment, the consultant's wife refers him to a family heirloom, in the form of a diary written by his grandfather, purporting to hold the leadership secrets of one Shaka Zulu, a true South African empire builder and legend (it's often very difficult to distinguish fact from myth when trying to study the Shaka Zulu story). The book contains certain principles garnered from Shaka's leadership style and it got me thinking a lot about some of the common problems we are currently faced with as a country.

The problems besetting our parastatals owing to serious management failures which have reduced our economy to a state of inertia, the challenges facing the supposedly corrupt, inept, and compromised (according to the flawed mainstream narrative) black managerial elite which impact negatively on transformation within the corporate space, the challenge of black excellence within business leadership in a society that automatically associates blackness with incompetence until proven otherwise(and that is a process that may take a lifetime for one to achieve).

One of the principles that Madi highlights in his highly palatable book (principle number three of ten), is that "to be a conqueror, be apprenticed to a conqueror." I was chatting to a mate over the weekend, who just so happens to be a leader within the Black Business Council, and we were discussing the problems they face in trying to advance the transformation of the SA economy and it struck me during that conversation that one of the things that frustrates us in our transformational drive is this lack of a conqueror's mindset.

Shaka Zulu was a ruthless conqueror who built an empire out of this "conquistador" mindset. History, the world belongs to those with such a mindset, who ruthlessly pursue their objectives and allow posterity and not their contemporaries to judge their legacy. This is why the likes of Cecil John Rhodes, Sir Ernest Oppenheimer et al are legends, despite their highly and rightly contested legacies. Black business, to advance transformation within South Africa needs to aggressively adopt such a stance and not wait in frustration whilst pointing figures at the government and big business. Of course, it would be interesting to juxtapose this kind of attitude with ubuntu philosophy, which tries to restore communalism and humaneness to all our social interactions and economic activities.

We live in a neo-colonial socio-economic environment, seemingly characterised by a comprador black bourgeoisie, ala Frantz's Fanon's cliched Pitfalls of National Consciousness in his book The Wretched of the Earth, because the people who built the economic system that we currently operate in, had such a conqueror's mindset and it's going to take a similar sort of ruthlessness at some level to reverse this unwanted legacy. I was thinking to myself, do organisations such as the Black Management Forum even think about developing a uniquely Africanised philosophy of management, as part of their transformational drive to change corporate culture in SA or is that considered a waste of time?

With regards to our paralysed parastatals, how is the Black Management Forum as an example assisting us with producing a patriotic, industrialist managerial class in the mould of the Afrikaner industrialist, Dr Hendrik Johannes van der Bijl, who founded two great SA corporations that are at the heart of the South African economy, Eskom and Iscor as well as being involved in the formation of other key SA institutions like Armscor and the IDC? It's also interesting to me since we are permanently surrounded by parochial ideologues on either side of the ideological divide, that Dr van der Bijl, one of the key architects of the SA capitalist economy in the 20th century, appreciated the advantages of state-controlled companies to drive economic development, but run along commercial lines. So perhaps state ownership isn't the fundamental problem here? Like author Philip Yancey, I was just wondering.

We need to see black managers rising at an executive level, with such a conqueror's mindset, unapologetically so. We need corporate legends of the ilk of American management titans, Lee Iacocca and Jack Welch, to step up and stand out in order to rescue our ailing parastatals and change the trajectory of our economy. It is easy to also forget that there was a time when the likes of Brian Molefe and Dr Dan Matjila were considered of such ilk, when looking at their current compromised status.

We have exceptional examples to look up to, the likes of Dr Sam Motsuenyane, the former president of the National African Federated Chamber of Commerce and Industry as well as founding Chairperson of the African Bank. We must adopt a conqueror's mindset to build and transform the SA economy and stop apologising for it and trying to massage unpatriotic egos. Of course, the other aspect of having the conquistador mindset is that conquerors are builders, who create their own wealth, their own corporations, and their own industries out of even seemingly unfavourable circumstances, conquerors are risk takers, conquerors are takers not receivers.

This is the type of go-get-it, ruthless, empire-building mindset that will be required to take South Africa forward, not all the rhetoric and dialogue that we seem to excel in as a nation. It is how the barbarians brought down the mighty Roman Empire and it is how we'll, in the end, destroy the colonial and apartheid legacy that we still wrestle with (despite what ahistorical denialists would want us to believe). It is the type of attitude expressed by the poet Robert Herrick that is required in this regard, "conquer we shall, but we must first contend. It's not the fight that crowns us, but the end."

Deracialising South African Society

The DA Federal Council meeting over the weekend drew huge attention, with analysts and experts predicting that the election of the DA's new Federal Council Chair and other outcomes of this weekend's meeting, will determine the party's future trajectory, moving towards a more classic liberal political posture with Helen Zille's victory in that regard.

In true South African fashion, the issue has in the end been reduced to race, with some saying old, white liberals wanted to take back "their party" from Maimane and the DA's "black caucus." Whilst reflecting on all this, the stark reality hit home me to again that 25 years into our democracy, South Africa remains a highly racialised society with race affecting almost every issue, evidenced by the social media uproar over the profiling of Dros rapist Nicolas Ninow.

Many people claimed on social media that there was an attempt to portray Nicolas Ninow as a victim worthy of some sympathy (this is where modernity's trend towards behavioural psychology becomes a tad problematic I guess) based on his upbringing, as opposed to a monster who raped an innocent child, something which would never be accorded a black person in the same position.

Juxtapose all this with the increasingly loud accusations that the

ANC has been fuelling the increased racialisation of South African society to deflect from its failings over the past 25 years. How true is this accusation ceteris paribus? (ironic, because they are not and this is the real challenge to deracialising South African society, but more on that later).

The ANC inherited a highly racialised South African society in 1994, with white privilege and black impoverishment being the order of the day. Has this in any way changed over the past 25 years? The ANC came into power under Nelson Mandela with high ideals of building a "non-racial, non-sexist, united, prosperous South Africa" that was for all through its National Democratic Revolution, a "Rainbow Nation" as some called it, but in order to move towards this ideal, the ANC was faced with the burden of dealing with the highly sensitive matter of a historical injustice against black people that needed redress.

It is an interesting side note that despite this high ideal of non-racialism and the ahistorical attempts of white South Africans to isolate Mandela's non-racial posture from that of the ANC and to posthumously claim him as "one of their own" who they would vote for if he was alive and in power, white South Africans by and large did not vote for the ANC under Mandela's leadership in 1994 and instead mostly went with their "swart gevaar" inclinations in exercising their right to vote in the first democratic election. What this in essence says, is that from the onset, white South Africans to a large extent never really bought into the ANC's non-racial vision.

The ANC's historical mission to deracialise South African society is clearly articulated by its former President O.R Tambo, when he said, *"We have got to move away from the concept of race and colour because that is what apartheid is. We cannot end apartheid if we retain these concepts."* So contrary to what the white South African mainstream would like to believe, non-racialism and reconciliation was not a Mandela project, but rather an ANC mission based on its historical values and vision for South Africa.

So, in effect, South African society remains highly racialised not because the ANC is fuelling increased racialisation to mask its weaknesses, but rather because the ANC government has, by and large, failed to transform SA society partly owing to the fact that white South Africans have never, even from the onset bought into its non-racial vision and as a result refuse to embrace the principles of historical redress that are critical towards deracialising and truly unifying South Africa.

The internal DA struggle that culminated in the election of Helen Zille as Federal Council Chairperson over the weekend got me thinking about all this, because at its heart is the issue of whether race should even be factored into our policy positions as we seek to move towards a better future. Zille and her ilk seem to believe not, and from the comments section of most online media platforms, it would appear that most white South Africans hold the same view. In his resignation statement post the election of Zille as DA Federal Council Chair, Johannesburg Mayor Herman Mashaba highlighted this particular fact when he said, *"I cannot reconcile myself with a group of people who believe that race is irrelevant in the discussion of inequality and poverty in South Africa in 2019."* In essence, the problems we encounter can be seen even in the results of the 1994 general election. White South Africans embraced the principle of reconciliation without agreeing to historical redress. They embraced non-racialism without being willing to make restitution for past injustices.

For white South Africans and people like Helen Zille, their attitude is that we just move on and pretend that the past never happened. They seem to believe that we can create a society of equal opportunity for all without dealing with the structural inequalities within our society that are a legacy of our divided past.

So, the failure to transform ourselves into this paradigm is what keeps us highly racialised and divided. We want the result of non-racialism and reconciliation without doing the hard yards to deal with structural, systemic issues that are inherited from our divided past and keep a majority of our population on the periphery, on the outskirts. It is this unwillingness to embrace this aspect of moving towards deracialising our country that has ensured that the ANC's transformation agenda has up to now been unsuccessful (yes, the ANC has also shot itself in the foot through corruption and incompetence at some level, but this refusal to embrace structural and systemic transformation to deal with the effects of the past has also played a significant role in our collective failure as a people).

So, the DA's current internal struggles, are just a reflection of the divisions within SA society and are just another indicator of how far we still have to go to reach the ideal of a deracialised South Africa, where skin colour does not matter. This type of South Africa would produce the type of voter who would think along the lines of O.R Tambo, who once said, *"I would not hesitate to vote for a White person as President if I thought he was the best person for the job."*

White Privilege is as Real as Black Tax

DA leader Mmusi Maimane's recent comments about white privilege and black poverty caused a huge uproar which once again revealed the cracks at the heart of our supposed Rainbow Nation.

To start with, anyone who argues against the fact that white privilege exists is guilty of the type of denialism and revisionism that the likes of AfriForum and Kallie Kriel are guilty of with their stance on Apartheid not being a crime against humanity.

A few years ago, I used to co-run a recruitment company for high-end finance professionals, with a clientele made up of largely big corporate firms specifically in the financial services sector. Our speciality as a company was in sourcing and supplying high calibre, high quality, skilled, educated, black candidates for our clients to fill vacancies that had arisen and help them meet their transformational objectives.

One of the interesting common themes that we encountered when engaging some of the candidates we represented, was how many of them would often want to leave a big corporate environment because they were frustrated. Despite being educated and skilled, often these people would hit a ceiling in the corporate space, and it would not be because they were lacking in capacity.

The white kid with the same qualifications as them, who came into the company at the same time as them, who happened to have the inside lane on them because he watched rugby and played golf with the boss on weekends, would be moving upwards rapidly whilst they would be stagnant with no foreseeable prospects for upwards mobility or they would just be given menial work which would frustrate them till they wanted to leave.

The issue with white privilege is that it is pervasive and accepted as the norm. In my recruitment company experience, black professionals would often get very frustrated because whenever they were put in a position, they would be assumed to be incompetent, unskilled, and lacking in capacity until they proved otherwise. A white professional on the other hand is assumed to be innately competent until he or she proves otherwise.

White privilege is also seen in the fact that corruption and ineptitude are assumed to be an inherent government thing (because the government is run by the blacks as our racist fellow countrymen are wont to say in their dinner table conversations) whilst the private sector is seen as squeaky clean and innately efficient because it is mostly dominated by white males. It is seen in the fact that there is more media noise when an ANC politician is caught in corrupt activity than when Steinhoff and the like wipe off billions of rands worth of value through corrupt activity.

White privilege is also manifested in that nebulous thing called company culture. Many times, in my recruitment experience, we would have a black candidate who would undoubtedly be the best performer in an interview only to be turned down for a job because "he or she doesn't fit into our culture." That is just simply code language for saying he is too black to work in our company.

I once had a client turn down a brilliant black candidate for a senior post because he did not have the correct accent or read properly, as he does not speak like a white person, we didn't think he was suitable.

White privilege is also seen in the inequalities between young black and white kids when they start working. I once attended a mate's birthday celebration, and the place was filled with young, black professionals who were still training to be chartered accountants within audit firms. The conversation turned to how different their lives were as compared to their white colleagues. Someone highlighted that the white kids at their firm all had cars bought for them by their parents when they started working or before and most of their white colleagues were living in apartments owned by their parents or paid for by their parents.

White privilege is a mate of mine "innocently" mentioning to me a while back, "but Mugabs, you are not like the other black okes hey. You are so much more cultured, well-spoken." He was saying that just because I speak English with a white man's accent and enjoy things that would be considered "typically White" in this race-conscious country of ours, then I am a "good oke."

For a young black person in the same space, however, you have to buy your own car and pay rent for an apartment, so the playing fields even at the beginning are not equal for blacks and whites she argued. That my friends is white privilege in action.

White privilege is walking into a clothing store and automatically being assumed to be dodgy, whilst a white person will never face the same scrutiny. It is my family once being out for dinner at a popular Johannesburg hangout spot and being told we are "loitering" whilst waiting for each other at the parking lot because we are so many. (What is that silly joke that a mate of mine once told me again: what do you call a gathering of black people? A crime scene. See, white privilege creates these kinds of perceptions).

For us black people, white privilege exists and is evident in so many of our ordinary, day-to-day interactions. It is a reality that we are constantly faced with and have to deal with. Of course, if you are a beneficiary of something, it may well be that it becomes difficult (or perhaps convenient) to overlook and downplay its existence and impact but for us who are on the other side white privilege is indeed as real as black tax.

The Psyche Of White South Africans

I have been deeply engrossed in a book given to me by a colleague at work, who happens to be the daughter of the author, the late Rev. Dr. Sandi Baai. The book, titled **Black Sacrifice: The Sinking of the S.S Mendi 1917,** is an insightful and thought-provoking reflection on the unacknowledged, uncompensated, overlooked sacrifices of non-combatant black labouring assistants who tragically died on their way to propping up the British War effort in Europe during World War 1 when the ship they were travelling on, the S.S Mendi sank in the English Channel on February 21, 1917.

Despite the noble appeals and protests of luminaries such as Sefako Makgatho, a former ANC President, to the British Crown to acknowledge and grant recognition to the sacrifices of these six hundred or so people who lost their lives seeking to defend British interests and in so doing chart a path towards emancipation for themselves, these honourable pleas fell on deaf ears. They were made to just disappear into nothingness as if their lives and their sacrifices meant nothing.

In remembering their hauntingly tragic fate, one is reminded of the poignant words of the poet S.E.K Mqhayi, which are referred to in the book, *"Be consoled, all you orphans! Be consoled, all you young widows! Somebody has to die so that something can be built; somebody has to serve so that others can live; with these words, we say: be consoled, this is how we build ourselves, as ourselves. Remember the saying of the old people: Nothing comes down, without coming down."* The unacknowledged, unrecognised sacrifices of those black people who lost their lives on the S.S Mendi, whilst seeking to defend an empire that did not value them, are a microcosmic reflection of the unacknowledged, unrecognised, overlooked blood, sweat, toil, and tears of the black

South African majority, which have over centuries built this country so that a select few can enjoy its choice treasures.

So, when reading the story of S.S Mendi and the black lives lost without any recognition or reward, one is reading a story that is the quintessential South African story, a story of unappreciated black sacrifice towards the advancement of white interests. To say this, is not, as some would arrogantly claim, to play the victim, but rather to reflect accurately on our history to more impactfully and meaningfully contribute towards its desired future.

Not only does the book bring out the subject of unrecognised black sacrifice, but it also makes one reflect on the converse of that, which is another unwanted pillar on which South Africa has been built, white superiority. Rev. Dr. Baai best captures it when he says, *"The notion that the Blacks were inferior is old and will not disappear today or tomorrow, it being firmly rooted in the political and social practice of White South African society."*

One of the fundamental reasons why the Rainbow Nation ideal has remained a "pie in the sky" dream post-1994, apart from sporadic outbreaks of "Rainbow Nationism" as best seen in the iconic 1995 and 2019 Springbok rugby World Cup victories, is that we entered a new dispensation post-1994 without dealing with this phenomenon of unrecognised black sacrifice and white superiority. We changed the laws and built new institutions post-1994, but up to this day, we still haven't found a way to deal with the unacknowledged black sacrifice and white superiority conundrum. This is one of the biggest stumbling blocks to social cohesion and a true sense of nationhood in South Africa.

Until we deal with this phenomenon, we are not likely to go anywhere together as a people. Rev. Francis Edward Paget, an English clergyman and author, who also happened to have been the chaplain to the South African Infantry Brigade in German East-Africa in 1916-17 made the following comment, having observed this phenomenon, *"The whole thing is due to the brutal, callous and absolutely ungodly and beastly attitude of the average White person towards natives."*

So, a large part of the problem with our dysfunctional "Rainbow Nation" is that white South Africans entered the new dispensation without ever having shed off their false sense of superiority. You see this manifest itself in the comments section of most online media platforms or whilst listening to most talk radio going to work in the morning. You see it in the lack of remorse, collective guilt, and shame that white South Africans carried into the post-94 dispensation over the dehumanising, debasing evils of apartheid, hence you find white South Africans proudly talking about how much better it was under the Nats in the "old days" and how this "black government" has ruined everything. Contrast the lack of guilt and shame by most white South Africans for apartheid, to the guilt and shame that the German nation carried for decades over the evils of Nazism, something that is equally comparable because both the Holocaust and Apartheid were declared crimes against humanity by the international community. White South Africans expect blacks to just move on and forget the past with its present-day implications because for them unacknowledged black sacrifice is the norm, which feeds into false notions of superiority. To dare ask the white South African population to reflect deeply on this and change their outlook as part of moving towards authentic "Rainbow Nationism" is to risk being accused of fuelling racism, embracing victimhood and taking us back.

So, until we deal with this white psyche, the Rainbow Nation will remain a pipe dream. To bring this up is not to seek to fuel racial tension but rather to embrace the principle highlighted by the brilliant 20th-century thinker, Reinhold Niebuhr when he said, *"If man does not acknowledge his status as creator, his freedom over the historical flux, his right and duty to challenge the inherited traditions of the community, his obligation to exercise discriminate judgement in re-arranging or reconstructing any scheme of togetherness which has been faulty in providing justice, he will merely become the victim of the past which accentuates its vices when it is studiedly preserved into the present."*

Rugby Is Our Game

The furore over the controversial Ashwin Willemse walking-off studio, in protest against being patronised by fellow Supersport analysts Naas Botha and Nick Mallet brought to light a few home truths about this wonderful sport that we all love, and which has given us so much to celebrate over the years.

To start with, I am a diehard fan of Noord Transvaal/Blue Bull rugby and Hendrik Ignatius Botha is one of my childhood heroes with one of my earliest childhood memories as a fan of this wondrous sport being his imperious performance in the 1987 Currie Cup final against Transvaal where he singlehandedly won the trophy for the Bulle scoring all twenty-four points in a 24-18 victory.

From there on, I was to become an uncompromisingly passionate fan of Blou Bulle rugby, with heroes such as former lock Adolf Malan, the imperious counter-attacking brilliance of former fullback Gerbrand Grobler, the elusive running and finishing prowess of the "try king of Pretoria" Jacques Olivier, the silky skills of centre Jannie Claasens. This was a team I supported and loved more than any other.

One of my most painful sporting memories remains the 1990 Currie Cup final when Tony Watson famously scored a try to win Natal's (the Banana Boys) first-ever Currie Cup in a hundred years. To see Wahl Bartmann lift the trophy on that fateful day at Loftus is a painful memory that will forever be etched in me. So, not to belabour the point, but my bloed is heeltemal blou and Naas Botha was one of the first rugby heroes of my life, with the "Naas is Baas" sign by a fan at a packed Newlands as Botha dominated the game against our enemy Western Province, being a particularly fond memory.

But for all this love for rugby and the Bulle, it appears that for us black South Africans, our love will forever remain an unrequited love as rugby people continue to patronise us and treat us as inferiors and outsiders as Willemse's very calm protest last

Saturday revealed.

I have a mate from varsity, who just so happens to be black, and he has a suite at Loftus. I would often go to his suite to watch my favourite Bulle and one time I remember coming out of the suite at half-time and running into a group of Afrikaner Bulle fans in the toilet and they patronisingly asked me as I entered, "When is the Orland Pirates versus Kaizer Chiefs game?"(The assumption being that I was in the wrong place as a black fellow because in race-conscious South Africa even our sporting preferences are racially polarised with soccer being seen as a "Black sport" and rugby being seen as a "White sport".). I calmly responded that I don't follow or watch local soccer and in fact, rugby is my number one sport, with the Bulle being my favourite team (the Blou Bulle Crocs, shorts, rugby jersey, horns and scarf I was wearing at the time should surely have been a dead giveaway). But this is the type of patronising behaviour we blacks who love the game constantly have to deal with.

In my other life when I lived in Cape Town, I used to live a minute away from Newlands Rugby Stadium and I would spend most of my Saturdays at the stadium supporting anyone who played against the auld enemy Western Province/Stormers. On one of these Saturdays, a female friend who just so happens to be white, went with me to watch a Stormers versus Bulls game and after that, she invited me over to her parents' home for a braai.

When we got there, with me fully kitted out in my Bulls regalia, the father was shocked and asked how someone like me could even support the Blue Bulls and what knowledge I had of the game anyway. We proceeded to have a long conversation about moments in the game from yesteryear: Morne Du Plessis' famous late tackle on Naas Botha in the 1977 Noord Transvaal versus Western Province Currie Cup semi-final, Blue Bulls legends who existed way before I was even born (let alone started watching the game) like legendary coach Buurman Van Zyl and Mof Myburgh amongst many others.

We spoke about memorable moments in Currie Cup games of yesteryear, and he was shocked at the level of detail I would have about all this. He expressed his shock that "someone like me" would have such in-depth knowledge about the game and then whipped out his old collection of videos (remember the era of videos?) so that we could watch some of those memorable moments we had been discussing. I was then told that I'm a "good oke" and "different" and should come over more often so we could watch rugby together and enjoy a few pints over a braai. See again, how easily do we get patronised?

I had the fortunate privilege of being at the UCT rugby club, on the day my old mate Luke Watson gave a speech at the Ubumbo rugby festival (a rugby club started at UCT by some of my mates to push transformation in the sport) on transformation, a beautifully inclusive, insightful speech challenging us to not see transformation as just a matter of numbers on the field, but rather looking to transform our thinking, our outlook, our perspective and perceptions as a precursor to actually seeing true transformation happen in South African rugby as well as South African society.

Of course, the person who recorded Luke on that night, ended up only recording and releasing the part where he spoke about "puking on the Springbok rugby jersey", a passing comment which was said in jest within the context of the speech, and which was so inconsequential in light of what Watson was discussing. Of course, what made the headlines and angered the rugby establishment the next day was just that comment.

We all remember the Geo Cronje and Quinton Davids incident with all its racial undertones. So, what happened with Willemse last Saturday is not new and is just one more indicator of the outsider status that we blacks who love and support rugby are always faced with and the constant refusal of those within the game to truly transform, to truly enter the "Rainbow Nation" and stop with the laager mentality.

Rugby is a game that belongs to us all and has the potential to unite us and help us build a better nation, unlike any other sport. It would be fantastic if the game in this country would live up to those words from the Rugby World Cup song The World in Union (who can ever forget that brilliant rendition by P.J Powers and Ladysmith Black Mambazo in the 1995 Rugby World Cup), "There's a dream I feel, So rare, so real, All the world in union, The world as one, gathering together, one mind, one heart, every creed, every colour, once joined, never apart..."Alas, so far, this remains but a dream deferred when we look at the state of South African rugby.

Mandela Speaks Posthumously To De Klerk And All Apartheid Denialists

Addressing the United Nations General Assembly, former President Nelson Mandela uttered the following words, which constitute the perfect riposte to FW De Klerk and his Foundation and all other White South Africans who are becoming increasingly brazen about their apartheid denialism as time passes by and the memories of the inhuman brutality of the apartheid regime seemingly fade into the horizon, *"it will forever remain an indelible blight on human history that the apartheid crime ever occurred. Future generations will surely ask: what error was made that this system established itself in the wake of the adoption of a universal declaration of human rights? It will forever remain an accusation and a challenge to all men and women of conscience that it took as long as it has before all of us stood up to say 'Enough is enough'... That historic change has come about not least because of the great efforts in which the UN engaged to ensure the suppression of the apartheid crime against humanity."*

So, apartheid was a crime against humanity, right? Case closed, no prisoners (literally so, ironically enough). This is true unless you are FW De Klerk and an increasingly brazen group of white South Africans with short memories and a revisionist view of history, who want to downplay the evils and depravity of apartheid, claiming that it was the Soviet Union and Communist nations who pushed through the UN resolution proclaiming apartheid to be a crime against humanity and as a result nullifying that very principled stance of the international community based on "rooi gevaar" (talk about being backward?)

The other claim is that apartheid didn't kill as many black people as Nazism killed Jews, hence it can't be put into the same bracket as a crime against humanity. Talk about utter contempt and disdain for black lives and the dehumanising, debasing, subservient, multi-generationally damaging conditions that black South Africans were forced to live in, under such a cruel, evil system. The sheer audacity, one is almost compelled to say, of people who should be contrite and looking to make restitution, but are rather growing more blasé, intolerant, and dismissive of black struggles that are a direct result of the inhuman system that apartheid imposed on them. It's astounding that black South African magnanimity amidst such a devastating historical injustice, is constantly confronted with growing white arrogance and a false sense of superiority in response.

This arrogant historical revisionism goes against the optimistic words and warning of Mandela when he said, *"This achievement is bound to last because it is founded on the realisation that reconciliation and nation-building mean, among other things, that we should set out to know the truth about the terrible past and ensure it does not recur. Ours must therefore not be merely a respite before the bitterness of the past once more reasserts itself.'*

It is only by acknowledging, embracing, and dealing with the bitter pill of truth about our history, that apartheid was an evil, dehumanising system that was a crime against humanity that we will be able to rise above the populist demagoguery with its polarising effects that we witnessed during the State of the Nation Address (SONA) last Thursday. To deny this history and demean the struggles of black people in doing so, is to create a platform for such polarising demagoguery to arise.

In Nelson Mandela's own words again, *"The ANC spent half a century fighting against racialism. When it triumphs, it will not change that policy."* The ANC fought to create a new dispensation where race and colour would not be a determinant of people's rights by promoting reconciliation and nation building, so that oppressor and oppressed could both enjoy the benefits of being part of a new South Africa, as was witnessed last Thursday when FW De Klerk, despite his apartheid denialism was allowed to sit in parliament and exercise his constitutional right to listen to the SONA, alongside those who fought against the evil regime he led, the likes of former Presidents Thabo Mbeki and Kgalema Motlanthe.

So there was no contradiction in the ANC-led state protecting the right of De Klerk to be in parliament and listen to the SONA, given the ANCs historical position, but the irony was that the beneficiary of such magnanimity in De Klerk and the many white South Africans that he represents who hold similar views to him, continue to arrogantly dismiss the extent of evil that they imposed upon this country by dehumanising and debasing black South Africans, in claiming that apartheid was not a crime against humanity. Once again, black magnanimity and forgiveness are met with white arrogance and dismissiveness.

This is one of the fundamental problems that keeps derailing the "Rainbow Nation." White South Africans entered the new dispensation without losing their false sense of superiority and changing their outlook/ worldview. Mandela spoke about this when he spoke about the significance of not just freeing the oppressed from their oppression, but also freeing the oppressors from their prejudice and parochialism. In Mandela's own words, *"It was during those long and lonely years that my hunger for the freedom of my own people became a hunger for the freedom of all people, White and Black. I knew as well as I knew anything that the oppressor must be liberated just as surely as the oppressed. A man who takes away another man's freedom is a prisoner of hatred; he is locked behind the bars of prejudice and narrow-mindedness. I am not truly free if I am taking away someone else's freedom, just as surely as I am not free when my freedom is taken from me. The oppressed and the oppressor alike are robbed of their humanity.*

When I walked out of prison, that was my mission, to liberate the oppressed and the oppressor both. Some say that has now been achieved. But I know that that is not the case... We have not taken the final step of our journey, but the first step on a longer and even more difficult road. For to be free is not merely to cast off one's chains, but to live in a way that respects and enhances the freedom of others. The true test of our devotion to freedom is just beginning.

In all we do, we have to ensure the healing of the wounds inflicted on all our people across the great dividing line imposed on our society by centuries of colonialism and apartheid. We must ensure that colour, race, and gender become only a God-given gift to each one of us and not an indelible mark or attribute that accords a special status to any.

We must work for the day when we, as South Africans, see one another and interact with one another as equal human beings and as part of one nation united, rather than torn asunder, by its diversity. The road we shall have to travel to reach this destination will by no means be easy. All of us know how stubbornly racism can cling to the mind and how deeply it can infect the human soul. Where it is sustained by the racial ordering of the material world, as is the case in our country, that stubbornness can multiply a hundred-fold.

And yet, however hard the battle will be, we will not surrender. Whatever the time it will take, we will not tire. The very fact that racism degrades both the perpetrator and the victim commands that, if we are true to our commitment to protect human dignity, we fight on until victory is achieved."

Racism continues to stubbornly cling to the minds and infect the souls of many white South Africans and up to now we have failed to liberate whites from their false sense of superiority and condescending nature, as Mandela spoke about, and that is one of the fundamental problems with the nation-building project in South Africa.

It has consistently and continually been the black South African who has been taking steps and making moves towards reconciliation, but this effort has consistently been met with white arrogance, dismissiveness, and false superiority as evidenced by the ahistorical narratives on apartheid that are now being advanced by the likes of De Klerk.

Of course, the easiest thing to do, would be to dismiss and ridicule these sentiments as those of another "incompetent, inept, corrupt, undeservedly deployed ANC cadre" (argumentum ad hominem par excellence), but in reality these are the sentiments that are held by a large proportion of black South Africans, even within the private sector, and to keep dismissing them and ridiculing them is to take the easy way out, as opposed to doing some serious soul-searching and seeing if we can change tack and indeed contribute to building a truly united, non-racial, non-sexist, prosperous South Africa.

The journey towards doing that is not easy, as Mandela warned us in the quote above, it is a road less travelled, which requires that we reflect on and address the "historical injustice" as Thabo Mbeki so famously called it with honesty, truthfulness, and a large dosage of humility, lest we give space to the opportunistic demagogues that we saw in action in parliament last Thursday to further polarise us.

The journey that is before us, which is "no easy walk to freedom" as Mandela also stated, requires that we embrace the paradigm of Russian novelist Fyodor Dostoevsky, in his timeless novel (not bedtime reading I might add), The Brothers Karamazov, *"active love is a harsh and fearful thing compared with the love in dreams. Love in dreams thirsts for immediate action quickly performed and with everyone watching. Indeed, it will go as far as the giving even of one's life, provided it does not take long but is soon over, as on stage, and everyone is looking on and praising. Whereas active love is labour and persistence, and for some people, perhaps, a whole science."* True reconciliation and nation-building are hard work, it's labour, it's perseverance. It is not, as we may have thought, taking one giant leap, as we did in 1994 with the whole world applauding us. Rather, it is a long journey filled with many frustrations with each other that requires the continuous sacrifices of "active love", and this is not something that is being shown by the likes of De Klerk and other white South Africans who continue to brazenly and unapologetically punt apartheid denialism.

Siya Kolisi and the Problem of Black Double Consciousness

The Springboks are in the Rugby World Cup final. An astounding feat given, where we were only a couple of years ago, so credit must be given to Rassie Erasmus and his team for having turned things around and made the nation proud, for having started a process and believing in it even when the chips were down and as a result now being on the brink of immortality, because in rugby-mad South Africa, nothing lifts the national mood more than a Springbok Rugby World Cup victory.

Some of us remember the iconic Rugby World Cup victory of 1995 like it was yesterday, still the best Springbok World Cup win in my view, not based on silly "Rainbow Nation" sentiments, but rather because in 1995 the Boks beat Australia, France, and New Zealand on their way to a historic world cup victory, whereas in 2007 the Boks only really beat one strong team, England twice on their way to a world cup victory and this team, if they win, will only really have beaten Wales and England on their way to Rugby World Cup glory, with the first game loss to New Zealand having guaranteed them an easier draw as they went through the tournament.

The 1995 Rugby World Cup-winning Bok team consisted of the spine of a brilliant, Kitch Christie-coached Transvaal team which swept all comers in winning the old Lion Cup, the Currie Cup, and of course the inaugural Topsport Super Ten Series in an epic final against Auckland in 1993.

As Springbok coach, Christie took the spine of this all-conquering team and led the Springboks to a famous Rugby World Cup victory in 1995. The 2007 Bok Rugby World Cup Winning team consisted of a spine of players developed by Blue Bulls coach, Heyneke Meyer, whose team won the 2007 Super Rugby title, after that sensational 82nd-minute try by Brian Habana, which silenced all my Sharks mates and gave me bragging rights even up to this day. That brilliant Bulls generation built by Heyneke Meyer did not just form the core of Jake White's 2007 Rugby World Cup winning team, but also went on to become a dynasty under Frans Ludeke, winning two further Super Rugby titles.

The current Bok team has no such characteristics and no dynastic pretences as yet, but they have the opportunity to make history and bring the nation closer together in a way none of the two former World Cup winning teams could, because in race-conscious South Africa, where even sporting preferences are still highly racialised with rugby still being largely seen as a white sport and football (soccer), a black sport, the image of a black Springbok captain lifting the William Webb Ellis trophy will do wonders for the fading claims *of "Rainbow Nationism."*

Amidst the euphoria of the Boks having reached another Rugby World Cup final and being one game away from being at the summit of world rugby, which we "Rugga bugger Saffas" assume to be their birthright, predictably the feel-good story has been about captain Siya Kolisi, a black South African who watched the previous Bok world cup victory in a tavern in Port Elizabeth because they did not have a TV at home. The quintessential "Rainbow Nation" is a South African story of a poor black South African who fought against the odds to come good and conquer the world.

It's undoubtedly an astounding and inspirational story, albeit unsustainable in a society where the majority of South Africans are poor and black and have to overcome insurmountable odds to attain any measure of success. We can't build a successful country, a winning country on exceptionalism, because it is just that, the exception and not the norm. (I am not saying we should not adopt and learn from the "best" in any way in case I'm misunderstood here) The Siya Kolisi story, whilst being positive and uplifting should cause us to reflect a little bit deeper on inequality and the type of society we are trying to build. Is it correct, that we have a country where young black people in so many different fields, careers, and sectors of society have to overcome so many hoops just to achieve their dreams, only to be further questioned when they get there about their competency, about whether they deserve to be there or are there as tokens etc?

In fact, by the time a black South African reaches any measure of success, given how many man-made obstacles they come across along the way, instead of challenging their competency and questioning their right to be where they are, we should be marvelling at their superhuman feat, refusing to allow structural and systemic inequality which constantly has them on the periphery of society to keep them from achieving their dreams.

Whilst pondering all this, I was reminded of a concept attributed to the brilliant 20th-century African American intellectual, W.E.B Du Bois, the concept of double-consciousness. In the words of Du Bois in The Souls of Black Folk, *"It is a peculiar sensation, this double-consciousness, this sense of always looking at one's self through the eyes of others, of measuring one's soul by the tape of a world that looks on in amused contempt and pity."* In these poignant words, Du Bois describes black people like Siya Kolisi's unique sense of alienation as they pursue their dreams in a world that is often defined by the "other."

Kolisi has succeeded in a rugby world that is still mostly considered "white", just like many black professionals, academics, business people etc. are expected to succeed in a world that is still in reality (again, I know I will anger people in saying this but we must speak the truth as it is before we transform it to what it ought to be) very white-dominated.

Within the perspective of this world that is still (whether perceived or real, you decide) very "white" in culture and outlook, blacks find themselves pursuing their dreams whilst constantly having to deal with this double consciousness. This speaks to the fact that they constantly have to view themselves not just from their unique outlook, but more pertinently from that of the "other." They find themselves bound by perceptions and stereotypes of the "other" in pursuit of their dreams, having to prove that they are not corrupt, inept, tokens.

They are caught up in this environment which only affirms and accepts them based on their *"respectability"* in the eyes of the *"other."* The fact that Du Bois highlighted this phenomenon in another century, talking about another country, should give us comfort that this is not a uniquely South African struggle, but rather the struggle of the black person throughout history.

So, in celebrating a phenomenal sporting achievement by Kolisi in willing the Springboks onto what would be a *"victory for the ages"* in the Rugby World Cup final and in celebrating what would be a rare unifying moment should the Boks win (holding thumbs), we should enjoy the moment that will allow us to escape the dreary reality of our everyday lives, as all good sporting achievements should, but in the back of our minds remind ourselves that we are still a work in progress as a people, as a nation and that there is much that needs to be done to ensure that the country can give the many Siya Kolisis of this world, in all corners of South Africa, a better shot at success in life. This type of South Africa would have Du Bois' understanding of equality when he said, *"the equality in political, industrial, social life which modern men must have in order to live, is not to be confused with sameness. On the contrary, in our case, it is rather insistent upon the right of diversity; upon the right of a human being to be a man even if he does not wear the same cut of a vest, the same curl of hair or the same colour of skin. Human equality does not even entail, as it is sometimes said, absolute equality of opportunity; for certainly the natural inequalities of inherent genius and varying gifts make this a dubious phrase. But there is more and more clearly recognised minimum of opportunity and maximum of freedom to be, to move, to think."* Then we can all sing the tune, *"hier kom die Bokke, hier kom die*

Bokke..." in unison. #GoBokke.

Springbok World Cup Victory and the Nation-Building Agenda

An epic victory by the Springboks in the Rugby World Cup final over the past weekend. It had traces of 1995 in how the whole country got behind the team and how it created a unique feeling of being proudly South African amongst all of us. It showed the capacity that we have as a country to achieve great things if we all pull together.

The Boks showed all the traits that are characteristic of South African rugby: brutal, uncompromising, punishing defence; set piece hegemony; dominating the collisions, excellent tactical kicking. These are some of the basic ingredients that contributed to the Springboks bringing the William Webb Ellis trophy home and the point to highlight is that this was the Springboks playing to their traditional strengths as opposed to trying to emulate the more open game of other nations, such as the All Blacks.

There is a lesson in that for us in how to become a winning nation in other areas, focus on what we are good at and perfect it, as opposed to trying to copy formulas that are foreign to us (we can learn from the best in other areas without necessary emulating them in everything).

Amidst all this euphoria for a country that was crying out for something positive to focus on, with so many negatives surrounding us, we can draw a few key lessons on how we can, together, build a better South Africa. The first reflection is on the thorny issue of quotas. Many people fallaciously claimed that the black players in the Springbok rugby team, who were deservedly part of the World Cup-winning team, are a clear vindication of their stance against quotas in sport or if you want to spread it further into society, against BEE and EE policies, which they see as discriminatory (I can already see you saying, there goes that Mugabe with his racist diatribe once again, but just bear with me for a second, before insulting me again as is your wont please).

My argument would be that au contraire, the brilliant performance by the black players in the World Cup-winning Springbok team (all the players contributed to a brilliant Bok performance but I highlight the black players for illustrative purposes within this particular context) is an affirmation of quotas in sport, of BEE and EE in the rest of society, because if it wasn't for quotas in rugby, I can bet you that none of these players would have gotten an opportunity to showcase their talent to the point that they shine in a sparkling World Cup victory and are seen to be there meritoriously, because they would have been lost in the system somewhere along the way. So, their performances at the World Cup show us that merit and quotas are not necessarily two, mutually exclusive, contending concepts.

It is because of quotas that they were given opportunities within the system and as a result, they were able to showcase their true talent and skill on the biggest stage of all, the Rugby World Cup and help the Bokke bring the trophy home. So, quotas, BEE and EE, are more about opportunity within a system that innately excludes and overlooks the black majority, than they are about discriminating against the white population. Hence quotas, EE and BEE are an integral part of moving towards a better South Africa, a non-racial, united, successful and winning South Africa, as we saw with the Springboks. These things are a means to an end, not the end itself.

Moving along from that, a post by a mate of mine on social media, got me thinking even further about lessons that we should take from this stunning World Cup Victory. Here's what my mate posted, *"The issue of unity and social cohesion.....sporting codes are but temporary aids to the agenda of nation building....you cannot expect a history of over 350 years.....to be forgotten because of an event.....! What matters more.....is what are we doing in between these events. Are we fostering a genuine national identity? Are we making initiatives to reach out to each other or we are waiting for another 4 or 5 years for another event....! The truth is that South Africa is a highly divided country.....we find ourselves within these imposed boundaries......imposed sense of* nationalism......and fake patriotism." Forget any spelling, grammatical errors, or syntax in this social media post, but there is much food for thought here in terms of the Bok victory and what it means for our nation-building agenda.

Despite the outpourings of patriotism and a sense of unity after the Boks pummelled England into submission last weekend, are we as South Africans truly a nation? Do we have a common national identity? Being such a diverse people, are there any commonalities in terms of language, culture, or economic life that genuinely bring us together, as opposed to dividing us?

French Historian, Ernest Renan, defines a nation as, *"an entity based on acts of the free will of individuals forming a collective identity: A nation is a soul, a spiritual principle. Two things, which in truth are but one, constitute this soul or spiritual principle. One lies in the past, one in the present. One is the possession in common of a rich legacy of memories; the other is present-day consent, the desire to live together, the will to perpetuate the value of the heritage that one has received in an undivided form."*

In South Africa, we know that our past divides us, but looking at the present day do we have any consensus about desiring to live together as a socially cohesive, spatially transformed, socio-economically inclusive whole, with equality and opportunity for all being the norm? The answers to some of these questions will determine whether this current Springbok World Cup victory becomes a catalyst, a contributor towards building a better South Africa or like 1995 it just becomes another memory that we'll often look back on as a moment missed, as a glimpse of the supposed Rainbow Nation which we continue to limp towards but can never quite reach. May we take heed to the words of American author Eric Qualman and not repeat the mistakes of the post-1995 period, *"history repeats itself because nobody listens the first time."*

Steenhuisen And The DA's COVID-19 Plan And Merit In Contemporary SA

Following that very insightful, exhaustive presentation by Professor Salim Abdool Karim, explaining in detail the government's evidence-based, analytic, and scientific response to the COVID-19 outbreak, I made a post on Facebook which got me into a debate with someone on my wall, that I found to be incredibly relevant.

On my Facebook, I contrasted the government's response as shown by Professor Karim's presentation, with that of the opposition Democratic Alliance (DA) presented by its leader John Steenhuisen, juxtaposing Steenhuisen's lack of academic qualifications with the internationally renowned professor, who is a member of the elite, exclusive Royal Society based in London, which boasts such luminaries as Albert Einstein, Stephen Hawking, and Sir Isaac Newton.

I used Steenhuisen's lack of academic qualifications to poke fun at the DA's plan all the while acknowledging that he must have had experts advising him of course, and strangely enough, a fellow comrade took umbrage with this, saying that my argument was ad hominem and not sustainable as the DA could easily have gotten an expert to present its plan, nullifying my line of argument. He also highlighted the fact that we should interrogate the DA's plan on merit and not "play the man", as I was doing.

He also argued that I shouldn't make it about education or lack thereof, as we as the ANC are the ones who gave SA an uneducated president in Jacob Zuma as well as many uneducated deployees in government and said that billionaire Johan Rupert is also uneducated to further solidify his point. You see, ANC comrades are not all people of groupthink as most on this platform fallaciously assume.

Anyway, my counterargument was that he was missing the point. The contrast between an uneducated, White DA leader presenting a plan and a globally acclaimed expert presenting the ANC-led government's plan, gave us a unique opportunity to expose the DA and White South Africa's hypocrisy on the issue of merit in contemporary South African society, and hence my line of attack was relevant and not ad hominem, in this context.

I argued that symbolism is important in politics and Steenhuisen, in the context of the contrast between him and Professor Karim presenting two plans, is symbolic of this white hypocrisy about merit in contemporary SA, which must be exposed, after all by default, if the DA was to win national elections, an uneducated Steenhuisen would be the country's president, surely a conundrum for all those whites who constantly dismiss blacks as uneducated and incompetent? It also deeply exposes the DA, who have been at the forefront of fighting for this supposed "meritocracy", that now they have an uneducated leader at their helm, but because he's white it appears to be overlooked or rather downplayed, even by the mainstream media.

I further argued, using an example from my days having co-run a recruitment business with a mate from England, which grew to include some of the biggest clients in the financial services sector in SA, specifically investment banking, private equity, corporate finance, asset management, mezzanine finance firms, and the likes. My example was one of these big firms in the financial services sector, which was known in the market as a "revolving door for black professionals".

The reason for this was, you would find many qualified, brilliant black chartered accountants or chartered financial analysts (this was the niche within which we operated, including MBAs and other relatable qualifications) coming to us from this firm, wanting us to find them a job in a different space because they were reporting to and being frustrated by a white Afrikaaner boss (this was the most common) who had been in the system for decades but was either unqualified or underqualified for the position they held and hence felt threatened by this more educated, qualified young black person to the point of deliberately marginalising them.

Of course, this calls into question how this unqualified or underqualified person got there and nullifies the argument often used by the DA and a lot of white South Africans about merit in our society. It is hypocrisy of the highest order and was a sentiment I encountered a lot in my dealings with young, black finance professionals during that period working in the recruitment industry.

Finally, I argued that to use Johan Rupert (I did not even bother confirming whether he is educated or not because it doesn't matter) as an example in his argument was rather narrow-minded because Rupert is the son of a great Afrikaaner industrialist and with his social capital from birth, it was neither here nor there whether he got a formal qualification to succeed in business. A story of a mate of mine, from a very affluent, well-known family bears repeating in this regard. In a drunken moment, during my days playing regular "pub golf" before becoming a teetotaller, he turned to me and said, "Mugabs bru, my pops made money so that I never have to focus on going to school like you okes. I can just focus on building my business and making more money." Talk about having brutally honest drinking mates, right?

Finally, I addressed the issue of Jacob Zuma, saying that comparing Zuma rising to prominence and ultimate leadership during a liberation struggle era that lasted for decades, to John Steenhuisen rising within the DA is the height of ignorance about historical realities. Anyway, by the time this was all done, the argument was no longer really about Steenhuisen and the DAs Covid-19 plan, as we had managed to digress so much, however, the issues raised remain profoundly germane even in a Covid-19 impacted South Africa.

3

STATE CAPTURE AND CADRE DEPLOYMENT

State Capture is not just a Gupta Phenomenon

In a presentation delivered to the ANC Gauteng Provincial Executive Committee (PEC) in 2009, under the title **State Power and Revolution in our Times**, Joel Netshitenzhe narrated a story of a senior civil servant who had been recently appointed, who was telling Comrade Joel that business people were approaching him and saying to him "en nou?" In other words, they were saying, we lobbied for you to get appointed to your current position and now that you are there, what are you going to do for us or give to us? Netshitenzhe calls this the "en nou syndrome", a phenomenon which is right at the heart of the state capture challenge that we currently find ourselves faced with.

There has been much coverage of the state capture phenomenon, particularly about the Gupta brothers and their influence on senior government appointments and procurement processes under the Zuma administration, which has led to a huge public uproar and rightly so. It is encouraging to see that the long arm of the law is finally wrapping itself around those who were involved in looting our state coffers at the expense of the subalterns of our society.

In looking to resolve the challenge of state capture within this new dispensation of renewal and hope that we have entered into however, we have to cast our net much wider than just focussing on the scandals and shenanigans that have revolved around the Gupta family in the past few years.

In doing this, there needs to be a realisation that the state in and of itself is a contested terrain, with class interests amongst many others contesting to find expression. Within this contested terrain, we as a government of revolutionary democrats are endeavouring to use the state power that we have enjoyed since 1994 to advance the National Democratic Revolution. This is in line with our belief that the state has a critical strategic role to play in society, with the state's role needing to be adjusted to suit the needs of the national economy.

So, in fighting state capture, we must beware of this phenomenon of political and corporate elites looking to use the state to advance their interests, at the expense of the rest of society through networks and patronage systems that foster corruption, in the manner that Netshitenzhe explains above. It goes without saying that this phenomenon is bigger than just the interests of one family, as the currently popular narrative would have us believe.

The fight against state capture is a fight to, "build a society defined by decency and integrity that does not tolerate the plunder of public resources, nor the theft by corporate criminals of the hard-earned savings of ordinary people", as iterated by President Ramaphosa in his highly celebrated maiden State of the Nation address. So, in fighting against the capture of the state by sectional interests, we are fighting for a just, equitable society where everyone's prospects are determined by their initiative, drive, enterprise, determination, ingenuity, hard work, and effort as opposed to their background or social status.

It is in line with this that we must of necessity build the capacity of the state and its entities to deliver to our people. As a governing party, we must systematically implement a cadre and leadership policy that will enhance our capacity to radically transform the economy to improve people's lives. This is informed by the view that we need a bureaucracy that understands its role as a critical implementer of the policy mandate of the governing party at any particular period.

This speaks to our much-criticised cadre deployment policy. The problem is not necessarily with cadre deployment as a philosophy, but rather with our current exercise of it. If there is anything that the Zuma years have taught us, it is that we must have a clear understanding of the relationship between party and state and not leave any room for a convoluted interpretation of this extremely complex, but critical relationship.

Concerning radical socio-economic transformation and the role of the state, we need to move away from dogmatic ideological positions and populist rhetoric and find a mean somewhere, which represents the best interests of the people. So, for example, our posture should be informed by the position advocated by comrade Joel Netshitenzhe, "We also need a mindset change in how we go about de-racialising ownership of the economy. We must accept that efforts to date have had limited success, and we need new conversations with all economic role players about how we radically increase the black share of assets and wealth. In doing this, we must be cognizant of the historical reality which shows that crude and aggressive indigenisation programmes lead to capital flight, declining levels of investment, increased social tension, and most importantly negative impacts on poverty and employment. We must also accept that indigenisation programmes often serve as little more than thinly veiled attempts of politically connected elites to capture rents (what the SACP recently termed radical economic looting.)

So, the battle against state capture requires us to do what President Ramaphosa has been talking about: encourage collaboration, partnership, and consensus building, a new social compact between the various stakeholders that make up our society, to build an inclusive, growing economy which is transformed enough to accurately depict the demographic realities of our country. In this way, we will ensure that no particular group can of its own "capture the state."

It is for this reason that we welcome President Ramaphosa's call for the implementation of lifestyle audits for all people who occupy positions of leadership, beginning with (but not limited to) the executive. It is only in this way that we will be able to decisively deal with the "en nou" syndrome that constitutes so much of the state capture project. In concluding his presentation to the ANC Gauteng PEC as referred to at the beginning, Netshitenzhe rightly postulated, "But I suppose we will all agree that if state power is to promote the objectives of the NDR, the response of a cadre of the movement to the question, 'en nou' would have been: 'n beter lewe vir almal' (a better life for all)." That is, what indeed, we are all about, a better life for all.

State Capture-An Alternative Perspective

Recently, I've been engrossed in Hennie van Vuuren's book, Apartheid Guns and Money, an eye-opening, insightful read into the inner workings and machinations of the apartheid state as well as the private and corporate interests that propped it up, even when it was supposedly isolated and an international pariah.

The book is interesting on so many levels, but one of the things that I found so interesting about it, is that it debunks the myth that corruption in South Africa is a post-1994, ANC creation because it clearly shows how morally bankrupt the apartheid state was and how it relied on a criminal, underworld economy to survive.

It shows how the apartheid state was dependent *on "respectable"* international businesses and individuals to survive, despite its illegitimacy within the global geopolitical order. It also gives one a window into the very close links between what we now view as legitimate business people from the Afrikaans community who now run businesses of global impact and scale and the National Party, and how state procurement was used by the Nats to prop up these business people and their businesses, who now funnily enough in their current role as *"legitimate business"*, are the biggest critics of the ANC government and its propensity to give business opportunities *to "cadres"* as they call it. As controversial author, Noam Chomsky says, *"for the powerful, crimes are those that others commit."*

As a final note on this book, it also totally exposes the myth that the apartheid state was an efficient, effective machine that ran like clockwork, totally contrary and superior to what we are experiencing in contemporary SA and the fallacy that many in SA today consciously or subconsciously subscribe to that corruption is a racial phenomenon (anyway, I'll save you from my *"irritating racial diatribe"* this week, as I know that's what you think I'm all about, so just bear with me a minute).

These are some of the thoughts that have come to my mind as I have been going through this book, but apart from that, one of the things that it has done for me is to cause me to reflect a little more deeply on the highly noxious phenomenon of state capture in present-day SA. It has caused me to reflect on the fact that, in line with the testimony given by Lord Peter Hain at the State Capture Commission a few weeks ago, state capture and the economic crimes that result from it, are not possible without the facilitatory, enabling role played by the private sector and big international corporations.

Without this *"massive infrastructure"* provided by the private sector, big business and international corporations, state capture would not have been possible, despite the best efforts of the Gupta brothers. As so aptly stated by Lord Hain at the State Capture Commission, it is these *"professional enablers"* who facilitated the capture of the South African state by the likes of the Gupta brothers and as a result, they must take responsibility for the damage caused and take proactive steps to prevent such shady, underhanded dealings from happening to the detriment of the innocent, taxpaying citizen in future.

As we look at the current poor state of our parastatals and the negative impact that this has on our economic trajectory, yes, we must apportion blame to the government for wrong decisions made, failed cadre deployment etc. but we must not stop there. We must hold the private sector, global corporations, and the likes equally responsible for enabling and facilitating the capture of our parastatals and sucking them dry to the point where they are now on their knees.

The collusion between big corporations, private individuals and families like the Gupta brothers and some politicians is a significant reason why we find so many of our government departments and entities collapsing, much more than BEE and *"tenderpreneurs"*, as we derogatively call them are responsible for this perilous state, we find most of them in.

If you don't believe me, then I challenge you to find out where the majority of the procurement spend of parastatals like Eskom, SAA, Denel, and the like goes. To the surprise of many, one would find that it is the big corporations, the established businesses that take up most of the procurement from state entities and departments and as a result, they are the ones most responsible for the corruption and malfeasance that has beset the South African state, and not *"BEE types"* or *"tenderpreneurs"* as is the common misperception (now don't get me wrong, they have also played their destructive role, but my argument is that it's minute when compared to that of big business and global corporations). So, we have to focus on and take action against these "professional enablers" in Lord Hain's words, if we are to reclaim the South African state from private interests and ensure that it does indeed focus on promoting and advancing the common good.

Cadre Deployment is Not the Issue

In his **From the Desk of the President** column this week, where he talks about building the capacity of the state being a key priority of this administration as we have just entered a new decade, President Ramaphosa said the following words which have gotten a lot of people excited, *"We are committed to end the practice of poorly qualified individuals being parachuted into positions of authority through political patronage. There should be consequences for all those in the public service who do not do their* *work."*

Many have fallaciously interpreted this to mean that the President is saying that the ruling African National Congress is finally doing away with its much-maligned cadre deployment policy, which is almost like a swear word for many in contemporary South Africa.

Firstly, this is based on the wrong assumption that there is something innately wrong with cadre deployment. For a party that wins a popular mandate during elections and now has to drive its political programme through the bureaucracy, cadre deployment is a no brainer. Cadre deployment (albeit perhaps under a different name) happens even in celebrated Western democracies, where a party will bring its people to certain key positions within the state, to drive its political programme in conjunction with the professionalised, apolitical (when it comes to work) career bureaucracy; based on the popular mandate given to it by the electorate. This is par for the course, in any normal, healthy democracy.

The second false assumption that is betrayed in how people have reacted to the President's words in the piece quoted above, is the almost universally accepted supposed "truism" that the South African state is in shambles and incapable of delivering because of highly incompetent, uneducated people. Well, I beg to differ. There are a lot of competent, capable, highly qualified, intelligent, and skilled people who helped facilitate state capture and almost collapsed the South African state. State capture, which set the country back, was not due to lack of capacity and skill through not having education and experience, but rather it was educated, highly competent cadres who facilitated and implemented state capture.

So, education and skill are critical in taking President Ramaphosa's "New Dawn" forward, but history has shown us that highly educated, skilled people with no moral compass are more dangerous to the health and well-being of a society than unskilled ones, as was evidenced during the global economic collapse of

2008 which was caused by highly educated, technically competent but unscrupulous individuals or by the VBS saga (the VBS criminals where mostly qualified chartered accountants, lawyers etc). Eskom also collapsed because of educated, highly skilled but unethical people.

So, education, technical skill, and proficiency are necessary but not sufficient conditions for building the capacity of the state. What is needed beyond that to enhance the capacity of the state, is what former President Nelson Mandela referred to in 1999, in a speech he gave at the Community Builder of the Year Awards, "an RDP of the soul for the moral regeneration of our society."

This sounds impractically idealistic and corny but is in truth one of the fundamental things that is missing in those who are deployed to the state, hence they are so susceptible to corruption and compromise at the expense of the public. So, the problem isn't cadre deployment per se, but rather the type of people that have been deployed to the state, meaning that the problem is that the ANC has not properly exercised its cadre deployment policy, hence the charlatans and unskilled people we've seen running amok within the state.

At its fifty-third national conference at Mangaung in 2012, here's what the ANC said about cadre deployment as part of organisational renewal, *"In the new phase of the NDR, deployment should always be preceded by systematic academic, ideological, and ethical training and political preparation. Cadre* deployment *should be underpinned by a rigorous system of monitoring and evaluation of the performance of cadres deployed and elected to leadership positions."*

If this is the kind of cadre that the ANC was deploying to the state: one with academic qualifications, technical skills, and a moral, ethical compass, I doubt we would have suffered the ignominy of state capture as a country and no one would be complaining about cadre deployment, but the problem is that the ANC hasn't been properly implementing its cadre deployment policy and so now society wants to "throw the baby out with the bath water" as the cliché goes.

Proper cadre deployment should enhance the capacity of the organisation to deliver on its electoral mandate through the state, to transform society in a positive and meaningful manner. It should enhance its capacity to govern and deliver on its promise to improve the material conditions of the people of South Africa, to be a genuine strategic centre of society that continually takes South African society forward, not backwards, to lead on innovation and technology to move towards the country's developmental aspirations.

So, what is needed is not for the ANC to ditch its cadre deployment policy, but rather that it enforce and implement it fully and, in this way, enhance the capacity of the state to deliver and grow South Africa in an all-encompassing manner that benefits the citizenry. In the end, as the ANC itself admitted at Mangaung in 2012, *"the neglect of cadre policy is at the centre of most of the current weaknesses and challenges faced by our movement in the post-1994 era."*

Transformation of Society and the Role of Cadre Deployment

As an organisation of revolutionary democrats that exists to transform South African society through the National Democratic Revolution, towards non-racialism, non-sexism, unity, and prosperity in a democratic manner, the African National Congress sees itself as the "strategic centre of society", which has the role of mobilising and transforming each sector of society towards that ultimate goal as explained above.

In order to transform society in this all-encompassing manner, the ANC then has to deploy individuals into various sectors and segments of society, who have the requisite capacity to promote and advance its revolutionary transformation agenda within each of those sectors. This of course necessitates its much-maligned cadre deployment policy, which has received much negative press in South African society, owing to the perilous condition of our state-owned entities, many municipalities, and government departments, all of which is blamed on "inept, corrupt, uneducated, unskilled ANC cadres" who have been deployed by the organisation.

What are we to make of all this and has cadre deployment been a complete failure? Firstly, we need to have a clearly defined idea of what a cadre is, because it would inform our response to this critical question. In defining what a cadre is, renowned Cuban Revolution hero Ernesto "Che" Guevara had the following to say, a cadre is, *"an individual of ideological and administrative discipline, who knows and practices democratic centralism and who knows how to evaluate the existing contradictions in this method and to utilise fully its many facets; who knows how to practice the principle of collective discussion and to make decisions on his own and take responsibility in production; whose loyalty is tested, and whose physical and moral courage has developed along with his ideological development in such a way that he is always willing to confront any conflict and to give his life for the good of the revolution. Also, he is an individual capable of self-analysis, which enables him to make the necessary decisions and to exercise creative initiative in such a manner that it won't conflict with discipline.*

Therefore, the cadre person is creative, a leader of high standing, a technician with a good political level, who by reasoning dialectically can advance his sector of production or develop the masses from his position of political leadership."

Looking at Che's definition of cadreship, in the Socratic manner of engagement, the first thing we should do in trying to answer the question, of whether cadre deployment has failed or not, is to ask our own questions: do we have such cadres in our midst within the current dispensation? If yes, are these the type of people we have been deploying into the state? If no to the first question, how do we produce such cadres in order to effectively transform our society for the better, towards our revolutionary objectives?

In the context of contemporary South Africa, one might see these questions as rhetorical questions, given the perilous state we are in, but the answers to these questions ultimately will determine the success or failure of the National Democratic Revolution. At its 53rd national conference in Mangaung, in 2012, the ANC declared the decade after that to be the "decade of the cadre" and committed itself to a renewed focus on cadre development as a critical part of organisation renewal.

As we are in the last couple of years of that anticipated "decade of the cadre", one would have to say that, judging by the state of the ANC itself and the South African society that the ANC prides itself on leading, this focus on cadre development has not happened. Hence, we can refer to the two terms leading the country, of the previous ANC President as "nine wasted years", most of it within the period of the supposed "decade of the cadre." So, if they were indeed "nine wasted years", they are more a sign of organisational and institutional failure, rather than individual failure on the former President's part.

So, the question of whether cadre deployment is a complete failure, hence the current state of our nation, can only be properly answered by looking at what true cadreship is, and after that, whether that is what we have deployed into the state. From my perspective, the answer is an emphatic no, we haven't deployed true cadres into the state. In that regard, cadre deployment hasn't failed, but what has failed, is cadre development within the organisation and as a result, true cadre deployment has not been exercised, because the people we have been deploying are not cadres by any stretched interpretation of the definition.

So, we need to go back and focus on cadre development as a revolutionary and existential imperative. This is the only way we can turn things around and build the kind of South Africa that represents our aspirations and ideals.

This, of course, is not a process that happens in isolation from the everyday, lived realities of society as Che so aptly and succinctly puts it, *"The development of a cadre individual is achieved in performing everyday tasks; but the tasks must be undertaken in a systematic manner, in special schools where competent professors - examples in their turn to the student body - will encourage the most rapid ideological advancement."* Ultimately, if we don't succeed in working through such a process, to develop cadres that we can deploy into the state and other sectors of society, we are doomed to fail.

One of the fundamental failures of liberation movements that became governing parties on the African continent, has been that they failed to produce cadres who could help them modernise and transform society, once they attained political power, instead they just assimilated into the existing system, in the manner of Frantz Fanon's "pitfalls of national consciousness" in his book, the Wretched of the Earth. They failed to develop and produce the "unreasonable people" who would take society forward, described by George Bernard Shaw when he said, *"Reasonable people adapt themselves to the world. Unreasonable people attempt to adapt the world to themselves. All progress, therefore, depends on unreasonable people."*

Cadre Deployment And Generational Mix

Addressing the ANC parliamentary caucus national staff lekgotla in 2005, former President Thabo Mbeki made the following statement about the ANC, "The matter of the cadres of the movement has always been an important part of what constitutes the ANC, of what defines the ANC." This is a matter that has been prioritised and of importance to the ANC historically, and in looking at the struggle of young people within the ANC to exert themselves and their "generational mandate" within the structures of the ANC and in deployment processes into the state, one wonders if it is an aspect that has been lost.

The recent provincial conference of the ANC in Gauteng, by and large, led to a generational leadership transition, with younger, more energetic leaders finding space within the PEC, and from that into the state, in the executive and the legislature, but the question that must be asked in analysing the efficacy of this generational transition is; has the new energy, vibrancy, and dynamism that is supposed to come with younger leaders being deployed into key positions and places of responsibility necessarily translated into a qualitative difference in terms of better positioning and capacitating the organisation to transform society for the better?

Of course, the same question applies at a national level, with young people having fought for greater representation in parliamentary list processes of the ANC and so forth, and with there being more young people in parliament through the ANC now, have we qualitatively enhanced our capacity to transform society as a direct result of that, or was it just a race to get into the state to transform individual and collective cliques' personal circumstances without anything registering in terms of societal impact? So, we have fought and continue to fight for greater youth representation and leadership through deployment processes, but what qualitative impact is this having on the organisation's ability to transform society and take it forward?

This question is germane because the central task of the national democratic revolution is the transformation and betterment of society. So, one of the fundamental considerations of cadre deployment should be the impact or effect it has on the organisation's ability to transform and build society.

Are the younger comrades that we have pushed into key deployments helping us bridge the gap (perceived or real it doesn't matter) between the ANC and society? After all, you can't lead and transform what you are distant from.

Are we punting younger cadres with the requisite skills to lead and transform various sectors of society, not the current anomaly we have where there are many deployees who would be unemployable elsewhere apart from the political context? So, for example, how do these people resolve unemployment, a devastatingly serious problem in this country, when they are largely unemployable, apart from politics? We are not calling for a "jack of all trades" cadre in saying this, but rather a cadre with expertise and skills which make them relevant and able to make a significant impact in various sectors of the SA economy and SA society at large.

In his 2005 address to ANC parliamentary staff, Mbeki spoke about the need to become "professors", and experts in various fields in order to be change agents with transformative impact. Generational mix, generational transition, and whatever other label or tag you want to give to the generational struggle, only makes sense within this context, not just about getting younger people into leadership and positions of influence.

So, the challenge for the movement is how to build a skills base that is relevant and can have a transformative impact within the complex 21st-century world that we find ourselves in. So, if we have identified a lack of skills as a particular challenge within this phase of the NDR, as opposed to dismissing people for being unskilled, what are we doing to skill them for the contemporary environment and its multifaceted challenges? A silly example is how many of our political leaders talk about 4IR but in fact, are clueless about it. In fact, in a fairer, more equitable world, 4IR would render most of our political leaders redundant, and useless, because they are so clueless about it, but I digress.

In talking about this new cadre, Mbeki also addressed the issue of "kgale ke le mo" politics, those who are wont to punt their seniority within the movement, the fact that they led before so and so and have been there for so long, as a reason to justify why they are most relevant for deployment and leadership within this current epoch. They use their "political seniority" to falsely claim relevance for themselves within the current dispensation (this also happens within the generational struggle of young people, as others often try to use their "seniority" over other youth as a reason for their relevance). In considering all this, one is left with the critical question, is this push towards younger leaders and greater

109

deployment for young people leading us in the right direction? We would do ourselves a great favour; if we reflected honestly and without "fear or favour" on this issue, because ultimately what we want; more than anything, are change agents who can drive our society towards progress and development, no matter their age, race, gender, or any other segmentation you can think of.

It Is Not Too Late For The ANC

It is January 1992 and Bill Clinton's campaign team is going through a very rough patch during the Democratic primaries for the candidacy for US president in the elections later that year.

Clinton's campaign has been riddled with scandal, moving from crisis to crisis to the point that even his team, who consider him to be a once-in-a-generation political talent (I am a huge fan of Slick Willy Clinton, pun intended, too, just by the way and consider him to be the best politician I have seen in my lifetime), are now beginning to doubt whether his candidacy will succeed, a state of affairs much worse than the fact that the polls were showing that his popularity was waning due to the scandal-ridden nature of his candidacy.

All of this was happening just before the all-important New Hampshire primary and for all intents and purposes it looked like Clinton's candidacy was over. Clinton, with his charisma and great political instincts, actually rode the storm and continued to campaign vigorously in New Hampshire and to the surprise of many, including his team, he actually came second in the New Hampshire primary, giving a second wind to his team and a second chance to his campaign, leading to him being famously known as the *"Comeback Kid."*

Clinton had announced his candidacy for the US presidency in October 1991, a year in which the USA had been engaged in the Gulf War, the success of which had given the incumbent president George H. Bush an approval rating of 89%, the highest ever approval rating for a US president at that time, funnily enough only eclipsed by his son, George W. Bush, who became president much later and had an approval rating of 90% post the 9/11 terrorist attacks (maybe there is something to be learnt there about the merits of war for politicians, but that is a topic for another day methinks).

So, Clinton announced his candidacy during a period when the incumbent was really popular according to the polls and the chances of success for the Democrats were seemingly minimal, but by the beginning of the 1992 election year, when Clinton's campaign was still wobbling and dealing with scandal after scandal, George H. Bush's approval rating had dropped to 46%, dropping to an all-time low of 29% in July of that same year. In just over a year, the Bush presidency had gone from the highest-ever approval rating recorded by Gallup polling to one of the lowest ever that Gallup had measured, proving once again the old adage about how in politics, a lot can change in a noticeably short time span.

In fact, Bush's final approval rating before the election that year was 34%, before he went on to lose to Clinton, who got 43% of the popular vote to Bush's 37.5%, of course taking into account that the US system works on the electoral college system as opposed to winning the popular vote.

I was reminded of all this as I was busy reflecting on the latest Ipsos poll here in South Africa, which was aimed at getting a sense of the political sentiment of the South African public at the moment, without in any way, by their own admission, trying to predict what would happen in future, with the 2024 national and provincial elections in mind.

The Ipsos survey asked a whole range of questions, which produced some remarkably interesting results, but for the purposes of this particular piece, we will focus on the main question and its outcomes. When asked which party they would vote for, if there was an election tomorrow, 42% of respondents said ANC, 11% said DA, 9% said EFF and 3% said Action SA. Of course stats and polling results can be interpreted in various ways, but what really stood out for me was that, despite loadshedding, the difficulties experienced during the Covid-19-induced lockdown, the ignominy of the Zondo Commission, high unemployment and the rising cost of living, a stagnant economy and the July 2021 unrest, if there was to be an election tomorrow, almost four times as many people are likely to vote for the ANC as the nearest opposition party, based on the survey.

So, despite all its obvious failings and despite the popular narrative (whether true or not I leave it up to you to decide), being that the ANC is a corrupt, tired, outdated party that has failed dismally on governance and service delivery and is destroying the country, the party would get almost four times as many votes as its nearest opposition party, if there was to be an election tomorrow.

Depending on how you look at it, this shows that it is not all doom and gloom for the liberation movement as yet, it is not too late for the party to get its act together and win back the rest of the electorate that it has lost over the years. Of course, these are not grounds for arrogance, given the diminishing electoral margins, but there is hope yet for the people's movement if it can get its renewal project off the ground and improve its governance and service delivery record. A lot can change within a short space of time in politics and with 2024 in mind, this needs to be the attitude of the ANC.

Of course, some media houses and opposition parties focussed on the fact that the ANC is going to become a sub-50 % party nationally for the first time in the post-94 dispensation, if the results of the survey hold(that is another way to look at the results of course) and the fact that the ANC is losing support en masse, which I am not suggesting the ANC should ignore, but given all of the mishaps and faux pas over the past few years, the fact that the ANC would get 42% of the vote if there was an election tomorrow, according to this survey, with the nearest opposition party being at a distant 11%, shows that the party is still by far the most popular political party in SA and that is the outlook from which it should work in implementing its renewal agenda and formulating a strategy for the 2024 elections and beyond.

One can also highlight the fact that if the results of this survey hold, the main opposition party itself, the DA, would have lost much ground when one compares the 11% to what they attained in the 2019 elections. Despite its many flaws in government, South African society is not necessarily rejecting the ANC, but what it is looking for is a better ANC in order to build a better South Africa.

The challenge for opposition parties, if one is to look at the results of this survey, is that they still have not convinced the majority of South African society that they are a viable alternative to ANC rule and of course, the collapse of governance and service delivery that has often been witnessed at local government level in the municipalities where opposition parties have clubbed together to take the ANC out of power, does the opposition parties no favours in the eyes of the South African public. The ANCs biggest challenge is motivating and mobilising its base to come out to vote, this means the party must address the disillusionment and sense of hopelessness amongst its core voters.

There is a wider disillusionment with mainstream politics and politicians in South Africa, which is part of a broader global trend over the past few years and this trend has of course led to the rise in popularity of ultra-right and ultra-left political parties when one looks at trends globally, but contrary to the popular narrative, there is much at stake for all political parties in SA, not just the ANC as we move towards the 2024 elections and beyond, even as we acknowledge that polling itself is not an exact science and of course polling results can be interpreted in various ways, but polling does help with both the science and art of electoral politics.

A lot can still change over the next couple of years which could turn the tide in favour of the ANC (both internal and external factors from a party perspective) because, as Vladimir Ilyich once famously said (I had to throw this in there just to agitate those who consider me to be an incorrigible commie), *"there are decades when nothing happens; and there are weeks where decades happen,* or to quote from the completely opposite side of the ideological divide (this is to agitate the Marxists and leftist types who consider me to be a "confused mix masala" ideologically), as former US Secretary of Defence, Donald Rumsfeld once infamously said, *"there are known knowns; there are things we know we know. We also know there are known unknowns; that is to say, we know there are some things we do not know; but there are also unknown unknowns-the ones we do not know we do not know."*

We do not know for sure whether the ANC will drop below 50% in 2024, even though it may be most likely and probable as things stand, hence we must aggressively focus on the renewal of the party, changing perceptions of it and its governance record with the public and rescuing brand ANC from the pits, where it currently finds itself. To be successful and turn things around, the ANC must focus on known knowns and leave the unknown unknowns to take care of themselves because as much as it may be a seemingly popular sentiment if one is to believe the mainstream, it is not a given that the ANC will be below 50% in 2024 and most likely out of government because as the Ipsos survey has shown, it is not too late for the ANC.

THE GENERATIONAL MISSION CAN'T BE DEFERRED ANY LONGER

In an article titled **Nurturing the Fourth Generation: Defining the Historical Mission of our Generation**, an article which expounds on Thandika Mkandawire's critical reflection on the first three generations of African scholars during the post-colonial era by adding a fourth generation of scholars (the new generation of African scholars), Dr Mshai Mwangola makes the following pertinent observation in arguing for the uniqueness and specificity of what she perceives as each generation's historical mission, *"whether we like it or not, each generation of people—and that must include its intellectuals as well—are born into a specific context that presents peculiar challenges."*

Mwangola further argues that Frantz Fanon, *"challenges us to the articulation of a collective definition of mission and agenda, emanating out of a careful examination of the peculiarity of the historical context within which a generation finds itself."* This collective generational mission must be conducted within the context of a generation that is, *"emerging onto the scene and still has a measure of control in consciously determining the direction its future will take."*

In a country where the unemployment levels are unacceptably high, with an economy that is struggling to get off the ground and a majority of the population mainly excluded from participating meaningfully within the mainstream economy, it is incumbent upon the emerging generation within the African National Congress to seek to chart a different way forward in advancement of the National Democratic Revolution(NDR), in line with the generational mission that has been identified as Economic Freedom in our Lifetime.

Looking at the South African body politic and internal dynamics within the African National Congress, one can only conclude that the time has come for the emerging generation within the organisation to take over the levers of power and begin to accelerate the advance towards a national democratic society; intensify the implementation of ANC policies aimed at materially improving the lives of the people of South Africa in terms of living conditions and quality of life; working with and amongst the motive forces of the NDR in order to advance radical socio-economic transformation, repositioning the ANC within communities and society at large as the primary vehicle for change and as an organ of people's power itself; winning back the hearts and minds of the motive forces of the NDR, who are the working class and the poor.

With the ANC and the country finding itself in the undesirable state that we are currently in, this generational mission cannot be deferred any longer, as an existential necessity for both the party and the country. In the words of the poem Same in Blues by the Harlem Renaissance poet Langston Hughes, *"There's a certain amount of impotence in a dream deferred*

Three parties, on my party line

But that third party

Lord, ain't mine

There's liable to be confusion

In a dream deferred

From river to river

Uptown and down

There's liable to be confusion

When a dream gets kicked around."

We must unleash a cohort of cadres from this emerging generation to take the lead within the upper structures of our movement in order to more aggressively pursue this transformative programme that is grounded on our revolutionary traditions as a movement, with the capacity to study, shape, plan, alter, grow, develop and structurally re-align our economy so that it serves the interests of the majority of the people of our country and not an elite few as is the current reality.

As a revolutionary movement, we must enhance and sharpen the institutional capacity of the state to strategically and decisively determine the direction and set the agenda for both social and economic development, dealing with our social contradictions in a manner that will reorganise society so that we are able to fundamentally address the wants and needs of the people. We must strengthen and modernise the ANC, both as a liberation movement and a progressive political party that is geared towards contesting and winning elections.

We have to deracialise the commanding heights of our economy and build an alternative social order that will ensure that the balance of power is in favour of the motive forces of the NDR. Of course, this type of generational mission need not create generational divisions within our movement and society, in fact, it will require inter-generational cooperation and contributions. To paraphrase Mwangola's words from the article referred to above, *"a generational mission need not result in generational divisions. The generational mission is not unrelated to that of preceding generations. It is a specific task in response to the peculiarity of the historical context in which its members find themselves, made possible only by the foundational work of those who have gone ahead."*

There is a popular and deeply entrenched narrative that the African National Congress has lost the capacity to mobilise the motive forces of the NDR and that the movement lacks the political will and boldness to drive the structural transformation of our economy in favour of the motive forces and it is up to the new generation within the ANC to rise up, take over the baton and debunk this false dichotomy through advancing its generational mission of economic freedom in our lifetime, a clarion call. It is this generation that must fulfil these words from Ayi Kwei Armah's novel, In the House of Life, *"Let us mix the long memories of a people destroyed with new narratives of our own making, as we move into space of our own choosing, as we dream in images woven from our people's best desires, as we plan on designs drawn from our own reflection, then make again the universe that might have been but was not, here in this place, now in this time freed for our new creation. Let us walk together, invoking the future into now."*

A Movement For The Renewal Of The ANC And Repositioning It In Society: #Adiwele

In 1992 a "New Democratic Party" emerged in America, with the ascendancy of Bill Clinton as the party's presidential nominee. Clinton portrayed himself as a different kind of Democrat to what American society had gotten used to, a centrist candidate who was more in touch with the voters who had deserted the party in the 1980s.

The image of the Democratic Party had been tainted with the American voter in the 1980s and there were preconceived notions about the party and its identity which Clinton had to overcome in presenting himself as a new and different kind of Democrat, different from the likes of Jimmy Carter, Michael Dukakis, Walter Mondale et al.

The "New Democrat" idea was not just campaign rhetoric however, it represented a new approach to governance by the party, something that had been stirring within the party since the mid-1980s. The story of the "New Democrats" within the Democratic Party in America, begins with the formation of the Democratic Leadership Council within the party in 1985, to rescue the party from the political wilderness, redefine its message, and, most importantly, win presidential elections.

This was an unofficial party structure that was formed in order to influence the party to move towards a more centrist approach, which would be more appealing to American voters and to break the Republican stranglehold on the White House. The "New Democrat" idea achieved stunning success in America during Bill Clinton's two terms in office and actually became a model for the renewal and repositioning of centre-left parties, which were resurgent in Europe and other parts of the democratic world as a result.

The story of the rise of the "New Democrats" within the Democratic Party gives us exceptionally good insights into the dynamics of intra-party change that can be used to help renew the ANC and reposition it within society. We cannot discuss the renewal of the party outside electoral outcomes and public perception of the party (brand ANC).

The "New Democrats" emerged out of an understanding of fundamental shifts in the American economy and American society at large, as well as demographic changes that influenced the voting patterns of Americans. An important element of the rise of the New Democrats within the Democratic Party is what one would term the redefinition of ideas and concepts that had shaped the party for a long time, this speaks to the re-imagining of policy positions with the aim of being more effective and efficient at driving socio-economic transformation.

The redefinition of ideas was one of the great successes of the" New Democrats" taking over the Democratic Party, reshaping it and repositioning it within American society. The "New Democrats" redefined their ideas to the extent that they found wider acceptance within American society, they were committed to reforming the party and modernising it in order to capture and captivate the American voter.

The Democratic Leadership Council concluded that the party's programmes and propositions were out of touch with the American electorate and that change was needed within the party, so they created their own intra-party think tank in order to draft a new democratic agenda and a philosophy of governance.

They developed a political and ideological manifesto in order to address the most pertinent concerns and needs of the American electorate. They developed a new progressive agenda to take the Democratic Party forward and reposition it within society and found innovative, new ways to achieve traditional progressive ideals and aspirations.

The Democratic Leadership Council initiated significant political re-alignment within the party. They adapted to the contemporary environment and transformed the party, advocating for government reform and reinvention. Their main idea was that of building an "inclusive society with equal opportunities for all and special privileges for none" and they had a reformist agenda for the state which, in their view, had to be activist in nature and impact, but they were not state-centric per se.

Of course, the difference with the ANC is that it still remains largely a party in power in contemporary SA, but the sins of incumbency have begun to creep in, which have created distance, whether perceived or real, between the party and the South African electorate, as evidenced by dwindling electoral margins in the past few elections.

In the recent ANC Gauteng provincial conference, a political programme emerged that has now transmogrified into an internal movement within the ANC for organisational renewal and for repositioning the organisation in society, which has the potential to have an impact within the ANC in the same manner that the Democratic Leadership Council impacted and influenced the Democratic Party in America This internal movement, an unofficial one at that has given itself the name #Adiwele, which is the title of a popular song within a local music genre called amapiano.

#Adiwele is an intra-party movement of those who are impatient for meaningful change within the ANC and society at large. It is borne out of a realisation that the motive forces of the National Democratic Revolution are demanding faster change and are starting to doubt the capacity and will of the ANC government to bring about this change.

It is about the fundamental, systemic transformation of the SA economy so that it loses its apartheid-era racial and gender composition of ownership, control, and management, shying away from populist rhetoric and cheap sloganeering which have no material impact on the lives of ordinary South Africans, but instead are informed by predatory instincts.

A 2016 article by Simon Roberts of the UJ Centre for Competition, Regulation and Economic Development, titled, An Agenda for Opening up the South African Economy: Lessons from Studies of Barriers to Entry, sums up the fundamental problem that informs the political programme of #Adiwele within the ANC and SA society, *"It is evident that South Africa is at a crossroads. Continuing straight ahead is not sustainable. The existing structure of ownership and control excludes the majority and provides ammunition for those who argue that in reality, the only way to gain access to wealth is through corruption and rent-seeking. Competition law has broken up cartels and achieved lower prices for consumers, but it has not opened up markets to entrants, nor can it, at least with the law as it currently stands."*

#Adiwele seeks to ensure that as a progressive movement that has been governing and is still governing, the ANC must set out rules of economic and social engagement that will advance its project of social and economic transformation in order to enable the quickest and most fundamental transfer of power from one class to another.

It is clear that the measures that have been put in place over the past two and a half decades have proven to be insufficient and it is important for those in the ANC to reflect honestly on this and self-critique as revolutionaries, lest we keep doing the same thing whilst expecting different results, the definition of insanity according to Albert Einstein.

The words of Mcebisi Jonas are profoundly germane in this regard, *"We also need a mind-set change in how we go about de-racialising ownership of the economy. "We must accept that efforts to date have had limited success, and we need new conversations with all economic role-players about how we radically increase the Black share of assets and wealth." ("Op-Ed: Radical Economic Transformation – a progressive...")* In doing this, we must be cognizant of historical reality which shows that crude and aggressive indigenisation programmes lead to capital flight, declining levels of investment, increased social tension, and most importantly negative impacts on poverty and employment. We must also accept that indigenisation programmes often serve as little more than thinly veiled attempts of politically connected elites to capture rents (what the SACP has recently termed 'radical economic looting').* "There are structural and strategic barriers to entry that prevent the meaningful participation of the majority of the South African population within the mainstream economy and these barriers need to be expeditiously addressed as an existential necessity for the health and well-being of SA as we move towards building a National Democratic Society.

There is also a need to redefine concepts and chart a different path forward as we seek to solve some of the most pertinent problems that we are currently faced with as a society, such as Eskom and load-shedding as well as some of the big problems we have been experiencing in our state-owned entities, which are supposed to be the primary drivers of socio-economic transformation and development within SA society, but have been terribly underperforming at the expense of our national development aspirations. Part of that will include rethinking our approach to state ownership, in line with the ANCs 1992 Ready to Govern document, which states that, *"State ownership is not posited as the in-principle alternative to all private monopolies: rather, this would be informed by the impact such ownership would have on the ability of the economy to address poverty and inequality and to encourage growth and competitiveness. Secondly, the developmental state should be responsible for enterprises that provide public goods such as infrastructure and basic services. "Thirdly, the private sector, including monopoly capital, is treated not as an enemy, but as a potential partner – and yet one that needs to be regulated." ("The problem with nationalisation – Netshitenzhe - Moneyweb") Lastly, balance of evidence would inform decisions to either increase or reduce the public sector while protecting consumers and workers."*

It is this kind of approach to addressing some of the challenges of our society that the #Adiwele movement is trying to bring within the ANC, with the aim of renewing the party, repositioning it within society and positively altering the trajectory of its electoral performance going forward, in a similar manner to how the Democratic Leadership Council impacted the Democratic Party in America. It is to address the despair and hopelessness of society, best encapsulated in these haunting, eerie words that were posted by a young ANC activist on social media recently, "to learn that the disdain for the organisation is no longer just on social media, it is a lived reality on the ground. The experience was painful. We are being rejected for things that have nothing to do with us, we put our own lives in danger for things we have no part of or understanding of. Yet our bravery is revolutionary. The more our leaders hide behind history and struggle credentials instead of accounting for service delivery or the lack thereof, the more it gets watered down in the eyes and minds of people. Our manifesto means nothing at all anymore. We seem to be too far gone as an organisation at this rate and the inevitable is all that awaits us. I suspect that even if there is a leadership change, the organisation itself has become undesirable for people to give it another chance. We are simply removed from reality. We remain an organisation of history and nostalgia. I could be wrong, I am not a prophet of doom, it is bad but hopefully, we will be OK."

Renewal lessons for the African National Congress (ANC) in the current degeneration of the Sandinista National Liberation Front (FSLN)

"The FSLN no longer exists. It's just an electoral party to put Ortega in power again." These words from the legendary Nicaraguan poet and liberation theologian Ernesto Cardenal should really cut deep for those of the left who grew up inspired by the Nicaraguan Revolution led by Daniel Ortega and the Sandinista National Liberation Front (FSLN) in the late seventies and throughout the eighties.

In the 1980s, Nicaragua, with its Sandinista revolutionaries who had taken over power from the US-backed Somoza family dictatorship, was a country that drew strong solidarity and support from leftists the world over, from both the developed and the developing world, with people mobilising to bring resources to this leftist project so that the massive literacy campaign would be a success and health centres as well as schools would be built.

The Nicaraguan Revolution had such a romance to it that many young western leftists even moved to the country to contribute towards ensuring its success, many even moved just to pick coffee beans (one of Nicaragua's best exports) in order to support the revolution in its progressive aims.

But alas, as we approach the annual Sandinista Revolution Day on July 19, Nicaragua's current plight and the state of the revolutionary party, the FSLN, reminds one of the exceptional literary work titled, The Autumn of the Patriarch, by renowned Colombian author Gabriel Garcia Marquez, where those who rose up against a dictatorship ended up becoming like the very thing they stood up against, or as so succinctly put by Albert Camus, the 20th century existentialist author and philosopher, *"every revolutionary ends up either by becoming an oppressor or a heretic."*

This is because Daniel Ortega, the revolutionary leader and hero, has undergone a "Damascus Road" type conversion (in the opposite manner in this instance) from being an uncompromising revolutionary to an oppressive tyrant, ala Karl Marx's The Eighteenth Brumaire of Louis Bonaparte, where Marx described the return to Napoleonic dictatorship in the coup of 1851 as, "first as tragedy, then as farce." Most of the Sandinista Companeros who led the revolution alongside Daniel Ortega have now been ostracised, jailed, tortured, brutalised and forced into exile by the government led by Ortega and his wife, Vice President Victoria Murillo, who are busy turning the country into a family dynasty in the same manner as the Somoza family dictatorship that the Sandinistas toppled in 1979 used to run Nicaragua. In the poignant words of Italian author Giuseppe Tomasi di Lampedusa, *"everything must change so that everything can stay the same."*

Legendary revolutionary leaders such as Dora Maria Tellez, a famed former guerilla leader and Health Minister during the Sandinista administration in the 1980s; Sergio Ramírez Mercado, former Vice President of Nicaragua in the 1980s and esteemed writer; poet and novelist Gioconda Belli who joined the struggle in the 1970s and became the International Press Liaison Officer of the FSLN in the 1980s; the renowned guerrilla commander Hugo Torres who tragically died whilst being imprisoned by Ortega and the Sandinistas in 2022; Luiz Felipe Perez Caldera; Luis Carrion and Leonor Arguello, just to name a few, long ago gave up on the party and in fact ended up forming the Sandinista Renovation Movement, which was meant to be an alternative that revived the revolutionary project, as opposed to the degeneration and decay that they had been witnessing in the FSLN.

The decay of the FSLN did not happen overnight however, as the party began to create a capitalist elite during its time in power in the 1980s, which used the party to accumulate resources and entrench itself within the comprador elites of Nicaragua, moving the party away from its mass-based political programme, despite maintaining the revolutionary rhetoric. To borrow from Ernest Hemingway's The Sun Also Rises, the degeneration of the FSLN in Nicaragua happened, *"gradually, then suddenly."*

With the party losing power in 1990, leadership squabbles and personality politics became the order of the day, so that, by the time the party eventually came back to power under Ortega in 2007, which it retains until today, the revolutionary fervour that had existed within the party was no more and in fact, Ortega and the party had been so captured by the interests of the traditional oligarchy and co-opted into its agenda that they made a series of compromises and pacts with conservatives and those on the right in order to come back to power, that one could say that the FSLN was no longer a party of the left in reality, even though the revolutionary lingo and propaganda remained. What remained, very sadly, was the philosophy of a revolutionary party without the revolutionary ethos and conviction.

All that was left by then was a party that exists to promote and further sectional interests and from that position, the move by Ortega and his wife towards autocracy and a familial dictatorship was a logical leap. Mexican poet Efrain Huerta put it well, *"As for my old teachers of Marxism I don't understand them: some are in prison others are in power."*

In reflecting on all of this, I was reminded of the words uttered by Dora Maria Tellez in 1985, when the Sandinistas were at their revolutionary peak, *"elected office is not more important than what one can contribute"* and I started going back to an interview that she once gave in 1991, just after the Sandinistas had lost power, in order to see if there could be any lessons drawn from the decay of the FSLN, for the ANC in its current malaise, even as it seeks renewal for itself.

In this interview, Dora Maria Tellez makes a few very thought-provoking and challenging observations, about the state of the FSLN after it had lost power in 1990 and what she felt needed to be done going forward, which the FSLN clearly did not heed and as a result, despite coming back to power in 2007 and still being in power today, there is nothing revolutionary about what the party stands for. The decay of a revolutionary party is a process, it happens over time and not just overnight, so my position is that there are some things that we can take from Dora Maria Tellez's 1991 interview that can help the ANC in its quest for renewal, so that it does not end up as a party still in power, like the FSLN, but having lost its revolutionary essence and thrust.

- The first observation I found quite interesting, was her perspective on vanguardism and the vanguard revolutionary party, which becomes the leader and know-it-all visionary of society, once it comes to power, something which she seemed to suggest had been a necessity when the FSLN was fighting to bring down an immoral dictatorship, but actually became a handicap once they took over power. In her own words, *"You know what the problem with revolutions is? The vanguard concept assumes it is always correct and has the right interpretation of reality, and that actions it takes are reasonable and fair in and of themselves. And since it is assumed that a leader occupies a given position due to a process of natural selection, by some nearly magical process this vanguard model takes the leaders to be the keepers of absolute truth. But nobody owns the truth; that's the first problem... That's the other problem. It was one thing to be the vanguard during the struggle against the dictatorship. But whether or not the concept of a vanguard in power is useful is an entirely separate issue— that's the debate. Is a vanguard party still applicable once state power has been taken? I don't have the answer, but at this stage, I think not, because being a vanguard presumes that society is in full agreement with what you're doing, and I don't know if that state of affairs exists."*

I really wonder what my ANC comrades, who view the party as the strategic centre and leader of society would have to say about this perspective from a seasoned, credible, tried, tested and proven revolutionary? To close off on this first point by quoting her again, *"After the triumph, vanguardism became a problem and the serious thing is that it continues to this day."*

- On negative electoral outcomes for the party, this is what she had to say, *"When we lost the elections—a phenomenon that was perceived as a defeat—the initial tendency people had was to look back on the FSLN's "happy times," like marriages that have problems and dream of the courting period. The only way to save a marriage is to completely renew the relationship, looking forward. Longing for the brilliant days of Sandinismo carries with it a nostalgia for vanguardism which, as I've said, played its role and was indispensable during the dictatorship. But its history after 1979 has to be looked at very carefully. All of this arises from the same confusion. We had hegemony, but we subordinated party objectives to the interests of the state institutions. Moreover, these state institutions even came to manage the interests of the mass-based and party organisations. The institutional agenda ended up imposing itself over party and popular interests."*

The party was too stuck in the past, she seemed to be saying. The obsession with the glory days and its majestic history was actually holding the party back from actually renewing itself. Forward-looking and forward-thinking is what is required to renew the party, as opposed to eloquent reminiscing about the glorious past. Also, the party had become so consumed with the state and governance, that in the end, state institutions and agendas ended up superseding and overriding the party's political programme and mass interests. She talked about a hegemony of statist thought rather than party-based thought, being one of the major problems. Negative electoral outcomes should actually force the party to look forward and stop taking itself back to its glorious past, she seemed to be implying.

- On the problem of linking being part of elected political leadership with deployment into state institutions and senior state positions, this is what she had to say (I know many of my comrades will not like this much, but here goes), *"The FSLN was para-statist and people ended up linking political leadership with state posts; that's why nobody could understand why a member of the National Directorate might not have a state post. But political leadership is political leadership; for example, Ricardo Morales Avilés was a university professor and a member of the National Directorate. But given this equation [political leadership equals government post], it was and continues to be unimaginable to think of a member of the National Directorate without a post. They had to be in some ministry, to have something! If that wasn't the case, there was real anguish: they needed something—a trinket to control, some institution, no matter what size."*

Here she seemed to be hammering home the point that being elected into senior political positions within the organisation (the National Directorate was the FSLN's equivalent of the ANCs NEC), does not mean one needs to necessarily be deployed into the state or given senior responsibilities within the state, one can stay exactly where they were before being elected and still contribute significantly and meaningfully to political leadership within the party. One can be elected into senior leadership of the party and not even be in the state, she seemed to be saying. Wow, wouldn't that radically alter leadership within the ANC? I know many comrades are not happy with me right now, but a party authentically seeking renewal, really ought to take some of these thought-provoking suggestions seriously into account.

- On the quest for state power at all costs, in seeking to advance the revolution, this is what she had to say, *"Power? What's power? Power is the correlation of forces. Who says that now the revolution can't continue going forward? What happens is that the journey of revolution in Nicaragua is extremely complex. It's feasible that this revolution will continue to go forward, as long as we set aside the obsession for power as a fetish and understand it as a means, not as an end in itself. Personally, the*

Nicaraguan peasantry's struggle has gone beyond my expectations; although it was counterrevolutionary, it took on the FSLN's political program. It's a revolutionary program, strategic for Nicaragua: the democratisation of land tenure and ownership; get rid of the oligarchy, of landowners, of unproductive big estates. FSLN's no longer in power? But that's revolution!! And if you don't get that, you're lost, you go on with the obsession for power as a fetish, an end in itself. Who says that revolution can't make advances under these new conditions? I firmly believe it can."

Controversially, for many who believe that the ANC should do everything it can to retain state power in order to advance the revolution, even entering into compromising coalitions with non-aligned political formations, she seems to be saying that in fact, revolution can be carried forward outside of state power, even when the revolutionary party has been losing the electoral majority or seen it dwindling. Basically, for her, revolution is not whether the revolutionary party is in power or not, but whether what it has put in place in terms of its political programmes and actions can outlive its stint in power and actually become entrenched within society. It is whether the political party has managed to fundamentally shift the balance of forces in terms of power and economic relations, which determines if there is a revolution or not, not whether the revolutionary party is in power or not. Hmmm, food for thought I hear you say? Fundamental change in economic and power relations determines whether there is a revolution or not, and whether the revolutionary party is still in power or not.

- On the drive for the democratisation of society, whilst maintaining a top-down, Stalinist internal party culture, here are her views, *"It's true that we had a pluralistic vision, but our concept of a party in power didn't correspond to it. We organised two elections, but still maintained the logic of one single party, with the conception of eternal power. We wanted to democratise the country, but we functioned internally in an eminently military style. It was all so contradictory!"*

Hmmm, what of concepts like democratic centralism and ideas of the ANC *"governing till Jesus comes"*, I wonder, in light of her thinking? Should the internal party culture not change, in light of the democratisation objectives? I was just wondering.

- ▪ Finally, there is so much more to write about on this particular topic but I daresay that this will have to suffice for now, what of the idea of the ANC needing to lead and direct every segment and sector of society? Here are some of her thoughts, *"Modernisation means going beyond vanguardism, becoming a party with a democratic vision and practice that accepts, understands and is thankful for the existence of an organised civil society, considering it an indispensable factor for its own life."* True freedom for society, would mean being free even from dependency on the revolutionary party, as long as the levels of consciousness within that society have been adequately raised, because as she herself said, *"The revolution is a phenomenon of consciousness, not of the state. Revolution is strictly a phenomenon of consciousness, and that's what makes it different from capitalism. If there's consciousness, it functions; if not, it doesn't."*

One would hope that this contribution, looking at the Sandinistas to try and identify potholes for the ANC to avoid in its quest towards renewal, would stimulate even more discussion and debate, not just within the ANC, but within SA society at large, because the lessons of the decay of the FSLN in Nicaragua, is that, even after it has lost power, the revolutionary party can still make a comeback and take over state power again, but in the instance where it has been decaying without any recourse over a period of time, it can easily take the nation down with it. Basically, a healthy ANC is in the interests of all South African folks, mark my words!!!

4

DEMOCRACY AND SOCIETY

Do We Really Need Democracy?

As we were celebrating Freedom Day over the long weekend in typically South African fashion, over a braai and some decent red wine, I had the opportunity to discuss with a gentleman whom I had just met, the crucial link between democracy and development which left me with much food for thought.

We, in the developing world, have grown accustomed to the developed world preaching to us the virtues of democracy, political rights and a free market system as the best way to ensure economic growth and a better quality of life for citizens within a modern nation-state. To those in the West, it appears that economic success and liberal democracy are seen as interlinked, with the former being seen as a direct result of the latter.

But how true is this? Does the Chinese economic miracle which is a direct result of a state-led economic development programme, led by Deng Xiaoping's reforms not show us that a state need not necessarily be democratic in the literal sense of the word nor does a society have to be open to produce the kind of economic growth that improves the quality of life and standards of living within a nation?

What of the example of Paul Kagame's Rwanda, a country that is highly celebrated even by the West when it comes to developmental matters, yet by all accounts it is an autocratic state where individual freedoms are subjected to the greater agenda of nation-building. These two examples seem to show that an autocratic state is capable of channelling and directing resources in a manner that produces the economic growth that is necessary to improve people's lives.

All these thoughts were inspired by this gentleman whom I met at this braai over the long weekend, who was lamenting the fact that our democracy in South Africa makes it more difficult to make critical decisions that can help develop our country. He argued that because our democracy requires consultation, consensus building, and public participation, often public decision-making is a long, drawn-out process that causes unnecessary delays which curtails our developmental agenda.

So, it would appear that democracy and development are not as interlinked and interdependent as the developed world would like to have us to believe. Instead, what seems to matter more than the type of political system that a country embraces is enhanced state capacity and efficiency in providing or delivering public goods, a culture of innovation, and entrepreneurship being cultivated and inculcated within a society, improving the ease of doing business within society and reducing the cost of doing business as they have managed to do so successfully in Rwanda, society being mobilised and galvanised under one developmental agenda, A concerted and targeted focus on human capital development. These are just some of the critical success factors that seem to be more important for development than what political system a country subscribes to.

The question that was asked is as follows: given a choice between political rights and better living conditions as well as a better quality of life, what would the people prefer? Amilcar Cabral seems to answer this question very well in his now clichéd quote, "Always remember that the people are not fighting for ideas, nor for what is in men's minds. The people fight and accept the sacrifices demanded by the struggle to gain material advantages, to live better and in peace, to benefit from progress, and for the better future of their children."

The people are not interested in political ideologies and systems per se, what they want more than anything is a better life and material conditions. For that, they are willing to make whatever sacrifices are necessary, even if it means reduced individual freedoms.

So, of course, the issue is not about a choice between democracy and development, as if the two are mutually exclusive, but rather whether the one, democracy, is a necessary condition for the other, development as the developed world has led us to believe.

It may even be more accurate to state that democracy itself is not a pre-requisite for development, but rather a by-product of development as societies that are developing often experience the phenomenon of a growing middle class, and it is that middle class that as it becomes more affluent begins to push boundaries seeking for greater civil liberties instead of being focused on trying to meet level one and two needs according to Maslow's hierarchy of needs, as most countries that fall under the developing world are currently experiencing.

Democracy in Retreat

According to a 2019 Freedom House report, there is a rising global tide of "autocratic capitalism", with it being suggested that countries where autocracy reigns will surpass democratic countries in terms of economic size within the next decade.

In a CNBC article by author Frederick Kempe, political scientists Stefan Foa and Yascha Monk are cited as claiming that, "within five years at current trends autocratic countries will account for more than half of global income for the first time in more than a century" in their analysis of an IMF report.

Prominent BRICS countries Russia and China are put forward as model examples of the rise in "autocratic capitalism" (in the African example, Rwanda is the quintessential example of this phenomenon) with the combination of autocratic rule and market-friendly policies as well as producing healthy economic growth.

Whilst digesting all of this, a few simple questions came to mind: if this retreat of democracy within a developmental context is going to characterise global politics within the next decade, then does democracy represent the highest levels of political development within a society? When looking at the health of a society, is stability even at the expense of democracy, more important in terms of enhancing economic growth prospects than building an open, rights-based society, especially in the short to medium term?

Is democracy and a rights-based culture a by-product of economic development and better living standards or is it a pre-requisite? These are all fascinating questions in the South African context with all our developmental aspirations within a constitutional democracy framework that values and upholds "consultativeness" to the point of at times slowing down decisive decision-making that is critical in driving and implementing developmental programmes.

Does autocratic capitalism enable a faster, more efficient developmental process and if so, what does that mean for the prospects of democracy within the developing world with all our developmental aspirations within the next decade or so? Given the choice between democratic processes that take longer and autocratic decision-making that is faster and could lead to more rapid advances in quality and standard of living within a society, what would be the preferable option?

These are all fascinating questions when one looks at examples such as Rwanda and Egypt, where the choice between stability and democracy in pursuit of a better life seems to have been resolved in favour of the former, with high economic growth rates being used as a measure to justify the choice. This is about as utilitarian as one can get when considering developmental issues, independent of any normative judgements.

Whilst reflecting on all this, I was reminded of the words of popular Russian novelist and Nobel laureate, Aleksandr Solzhenitsyn in his essay Rebuilding Russia: Reflections and Tentative Proposals, outlining his thoughts on the political and economic choices facing post-Communist Russia, "Human rights are a fine thing, but how can we make ourselves sure that our rights do not expand at the expense of the rights of others. A society with unlimited rights is incapable of standing up to adversity. If we do not wish to be ruled by a coercive authority, then each of us must rein himself in... A stable society is achieved not by balancing opposing forces but by conscious self-limitation: by the principle that we are always duty-bound to defer to the sense of moral justice."

All these thoughts led one to conclude that in terms of the democracy/developmental conundrum, there are no clear-cut answers, as diverse examples and case studies could be put forward to advance a particular view, based on one's pre-determined inclinations. In the South African context, with the governing party pursuing what is termed a National Democratic Revolution, one wonders whether the National Democratic Revolution would be more speedily advanced if there were not so many democratic loopholes to jump over in the quest towards building a national democratic society.

Coalitions are a Bottleneck

The 2016 local government elections introduced a novel dynamic into South African politics with coalition politics becoming a prominent feature within the local government terrain. Looking at the perilous state of the City of Johannesburg, with the municipality in financial shambles and service delivery at an all-time low, one wonders if the outcome did indeed enhance democracy from the perspective of the ordinary citizen.

The give-and-take nature of coalition politics has seemingly introduced a state of paralysis when it comes to decision-making and stability within our municipalities which has had a negative impact on service delivery, as our municipalities are even failing to deliver services at a basic level, such as waste collection and maintenance of basic infrastructure.

These bipartisan political arrangements which are not based on any ideological congruence or a sound political programme, but rather on convenience and expediency have had a disastrous impact on the quest to materially improve the lives of ordinary citizens. They reinforce the point highlighted by political scientist, Professor Mark L. Haas when he states that, "a number of key historical and contemporary cases demonstrate how difficult it is for ideological enemies to overcome the impediments to alignment created by their ideological differences."

Can a proper political programme be executed when there is no ideological alignment within a governing coalition? In fact, within the contemporary political realm, does ideology in and of itself even matter or are we just caught up in an irreversible race to the bottom with catastrophic entropy levels being the new norm and the interests of the political elite trumping those of the public? It would then appear that these coalition arrangements that are a result of the 2016 local government elections are themselves a bottleneck to service delivery and good governance.

In his widely read book, The Goal, business management guru Eliyahu M. Goldratt postulates that the "capacity of any manufacturing plant is equal to the capacity of its bottlenecks", and his thinking has been used to deal with organisational inefficiencies at various societal levels the world over. One wonders how this principle itself would find expression at the local government level where the politics of coalitions, with all the wheeling and dealing involved behind the scenes have proven to be a huge hindrance to quality service delivery.

If anything, what we have witnessed at a local government level since 2016 is evidence of the fact that promoting political pluralism within a society does not necessarily equate to strengthening democracy, especially when such pluralism does not enhance or promote a people-centred ethos within the body politic. After all, the positive enhancement of the lived experiences of the governed should be the ultimate end goal of democratic politics, not the protection of the interests of an oligarchic political elite, which is what we are currently witnessing through our coalitions at the municipal level in South African politics.

Perhaps going forward, without necessarily degenerating into a winner-takes-all, first-past-the-post politics, we need to ensure that we give an individual political organisation a decisive electoral mandate to go and implement their political programme and then based on the scorecard set for themselves through their manifesto, we can then determine whether they are worthy of still governing us after every five-year term has ended. This in my perspective, would produce greater political accountability than the chaos that coalition politics are producing at the municipal level as things stand.

So, as we move towards local government elections in 2021 and beyond, we need to become more decisive as an electorate and then through that create better conditions to hold our public representatives accountable. It is after all, the indecisiveness of the electorate as well which produced the inconclusive results of the 2016 local government elections, which have led to this unwanted phenomenon of coalition politics and the resultant state of inertia, that we find our municipalities caught in.

Local Government-The Coalface of our Democracy

With local government being the coal face of all human development activities, the perilous state of most of our municipalities around the country is a window into the ill-health of our society, which demands urgent attention and intervention, if we are ever going to achieve our developmental objectives as a people.

In the Free State, we were recently awakened to the reality of the provincial government placing Mangaung municipality under administration. In Gauteng, we are still to get a full picture of the mess that Herman Mashaba left the City of Johannesburg in, but the evidence is there for us all to see in mushrooming potholes everywhere, traffic lights not working, rubbish not being collected, and neighbourhoods looking like dumping sites and of course perpetual water and power outages.

The less said about Tshwane Municipality, which has been put under administration by the provincial government, the better, with even basic services such as water proving too much for the municipality to provide to the extent that even the Human Rights Commission had to step in. Looking further afield to the Eastern Cape, one needs only look at the complete shambles that is Nelson Mandela Bay Municipality to realise that we are in serious trouble as a people and reading through Cristian Olver's eye-witness account of the rot within that municipality, How to Steal a City, leaves one with a serious sense of foreboding.

These are all issues that need to be tackled in a non-partisan manner because it is largely the partisan nature of our politics at a local government level, that has left service delivery in a state of inertia with entropy reigning and the interests of citizens being negatively affected.

In reflecting upon all this, one was reminded of the words of renowned poet Walt Whitman, in his poem lamenting the state of affairs in his country at the time titled, To The State, *"Why reclining, interrogating? Why myself and all drowsing?*

What deepening twilight—scum floating atop of the waters,

Who are they as bats and night dogs askant in the capitol?

What a filthy Presidentiad! (O South, your torrid suns! O North, your arctic freezings!)

Are those really Congressmen? Are those the great Judges? Is that the President?

Then I will sleep awhile yet, for I see that these States sleep, for reasons"

Addressing an eThekwini Metro leadership breakfast session, in a 2015 speech with the profoundly germane theme, *Building a*

Capable Municipality: How to Lead in a Politically Charged Environment, Mapungubwe Institute for Strategic Reflection Executive Director, Joel Netshitenzhe, made the following pertinent observations in seeking to provide solutions for the local government conundrum that we are faced with:

- The bureaucracy forms a critical part of the state: it is the infrastructure through which policy and technical imperatives find concrete expression. It is not apolitical, as it is meant to carry out the policy mandate of the party that wins elections. It should be non-partisan, but its functions are essentially political.

- We should always avoid conflating the party, the government and the state. While the bureaucracy is obliged to carry out the popular mandate as directed by the ruling party in any specific sphere, it has a broader responsibility to society; in relation to the burghers of eThekwini (or any particular municipality)– from big and small business to workers and the unemployed – on matters pertaining to the provision of municipal services.

- A critical element of this is the basic principle that governance should be based on clear rules which everyone must observe; and that there should be accountability – both upwards to relevant supervisors and downwards to staff and society in general – on the part both of the bureaucracy and the political principals.

- The bureaucracy should enjoy 'embedded autonomy': it should be networked in society to be able to give leadership to economic development, but it should be autonomous of any special interests.

- The bureaucracy should be staffed by competent, mission-oriented professionals, and it should be "sufficiently insulated from the push and pull of special short-term interests", corruption, and political favours.

- The personnel should be career bureaucrats, with the primary mode of recruitment and promotion being merit rather than political or personal connections. Expertise and competence should be highly prized and rewarded, and an independent perspective – as advisors to the political principals – should be cultivated.

- The bureaucracy should be non-partisan, but it is never apolitical as everything it does relates to politics in the broader sense.

To highlight this final point, Netshitenzhe gives an example of the UK, where during elections, political parties all release their manifestos, which are in essence, their contract with the people who vote for them, *"the bureaucracy develops detailed plans on how the manifestos of at least the largest parties can be operationalised. This is crucial for the practical reason that a new government should able to hit the ground running, but it also entrenches a culture to ensure clear dove-tailing between bureaucratic pursuits and the popular mandate."*

These are all very important principles that we must endorse if we want to further enhance the efficacy of our municipalities and ensure that they can deliver on their Section 152 responsibilities, as it is the highly politicised and partisan nature of local government that is creating service delivery deficits that are a serious threat to the health of our democracy.

It is these highly politicised and partisan local politics that have produced coalition governments and arrangements within our municipalities that advance narrow individual and party interests, with no regard whatsoever towards their Section 152 responsibilities, with the outcome being political instability that has a devastatingly negative impact on quality of life for ordinary citizens.

We must fix local government if we are serious about enhancing the capacity of the state to be developmental and impactful in aims and output, with the ultimate objective of improving the living conditions and quality of life of ordinary citizens, in line with the words once uttered by the Roman Senator, Marcus Tullius Cicero, *"the good life is impossible without a good state; and there is no greater blessing than a well-ordered state."*

The Rise of Populism

Following the ascendancy of Boris Johnson to the position of Prime Minister of Britain, there has been much alarm expressed by the chattering classes and our erstwhile social media analysts about the seemingly undesirable rise of populism and populist politics within the global political arena. Johnson's stepping into office at Number 10 Downing Street with its Brexit implications presents further evidence of the right-wing, conservative advance (and the retreat of liberalism) within the global body politic that I wrote about a couple of weeks ago. Not only that, but it also showcases the clear historical link between populism with its "Trumpean" characteristics in the current epoch and extreme nationalism, a topic and opinion piece on its own for another day, I guess.

The interesting thing about this phenomenon is that it cuts across both sides of the ideological terrain. We have Donald Trump and Boris Johnson on the right and Bernie Sanders and Jeremy Corbyn on the left, all populists tapping into the popular dissent with the current socio-economic climate, which advances the interests of an "oligarchic elite" at the expense of the common man, the ordinary citizen, the subalterns of society or in Fanonian phraseology "The Wretched of the Earth."

So, it would appear that populism, with its innate characteristics, has no ideological biases unlike most of us who look at issues through the parochial lenses of our dogmatic ideological leanings. In considering all this, my point of departure was that populism is not a new or novel phenomenon within the global political arena, rather it is to some extent "the essence of the quintessence" of modern, popular (there is a reason why it is called that) democracy with all its idiosyncrasies.

Politics, after all, is about the contestation of power and within the modern, democratic framework the person or party that wins the "popular vote" in the end attains the power that is needed to advance a certain political programme or agenda. (Although, this "popular vote" phenomenon did not work for Hillary Clinton in the context of the American electoral college system). So, populism is by definition a permanent feature of democratic politics, not a recent, unwanted phenomenon.

The best politicians throughout history have used populist appeals to advance themselves and whatever agendas they espouse, whether right or wrong. Hence, Adolf Hitler, one of the greatest orators in history, was a brilliant politician. At this point, I must put forward the disclaimer that this is an objective analysis of Hitler the politician's modus operandi to attain and retain power through populist, nationalist appeal within the modern political context, not a normative approval of his warped, evil ideas lest I end up in trouble like a mate of mine who is a prominent #FeesMustFall leader in this country.

In any case, the question of evil is best approached within the nuanced perspective advanced by Russian novelist Aleksandr Solzhenitsyn in his The Gulag Archipelago, which reflects on the rampant evils of Stalinist Russia, "if only there were evil people somewhere insidiously committing evil deeds, and it were necessary only to separate them from the rest of us and destroy them. But the line dividing good and evil cuts through the heart of every human being. And who is willing to destroy a piece of his own heart? During the life of any heart, this line keeps changing place; sometimes it is squeezed one way by exuberant evil and sometimes it shifts to allow enough space for good to flourish. The same human being is at various ages, under various circumstances, a different human being. At times he is close to being a devil, and at times sainthood. But his name doesn't change, and to that name, we ascribe the whole lot, good and evil." Dr Ravi Zacharias, a renowned author and public speaker also has an interesting outlook when deciphering the question of evil in the context of analysing human behaviour, history and society at large, but I'm aware that this may be a bit too much to swallow in our highly polarised, social media age, but I digress.

Democratic politics and populism go hand in hand. It is only those who can appeal to the heart issues, the felt needs and fears of society who can successfully attain power within a democratic dispensation. For a deeper analysis of this, one needs to read Drew Westen's brilliant book, The Political Brain: The Role of Emotion in Deciding the Fate of the Nation. It is through populist appeal that Sir Winston Churchill kept the British public's hopes up in their fight against the evils of Nazism, hence his brilliance.

One of the greatest politicians in history, the Roman Senator Marcus Tullius Cicero, also renowned as one of history's great orators understood the power of populist appeal in the art of politics and politicking. Karl Rove, a brilliant right-wing, conservative political strategist and the many conservative think tanks in the USA also understand this and hence their many electoral successes. Karl Rove and the many conservative think tanks in the USA disprove the misnomer that populism equals or results in/from anti-intellectualism. Again, this is not a normative statement on Karl Rove's politics but rather an objective statement looking at his politics' efficacy in terms of electoral outcomes. It was the renowned former New York Governor, Mario Cuomo after all who coined the well-known and overused phrase, "You campaign in poetry. You govern in prose" out of an understanding of the power of populist appeal in democratic politics.

Campaign Funding is a Form of Lobbying

Following the recent leaks of bank statements revealing that some high-profile ANC politicians and members of the executive, alliance leaders and ANC members and leaders received financial disbursements as part of President Matamela Ramaphosa's 2017 campaign for the ANC presidency, there has been much uproar, with a call for certain cabinet ministers to be removed who allegedly benefitted financially from their support for Ramaphosa.

It appears that the campaign to portray President Ramaphosa as a "typically corrupt ANC politician" who offers nothing new with his "New Dawn" has gained momentum with all these revelations that have found much mileage on social media platforms. In reflecting upon this brouhaha, one was left with a few obvious questions. Is there anything innately wrong with using money within a political campaign (whether an internal party or external contest) to enable one to win a political contest?

What, if anything, is wrong with individuals or groups being given money and resources to go and promote a certain political perspective or view within the context of a political campaign? I mean, politics is about the contestation of power and within that, there are different class and stakeholder interests represented, so why do we naively assume that money won't be involved in this contestation of diverse and divergent interests?

In the interests of fairness and the spirit of democracy, one would of course need to somehow regulate this aspect of a political campaign, to ensure that divergent views have an equal chance of succeeding, but that does not in any way imply the complete exclusion of money as a facilitatory lobbying tool in campaigning.

To dismiss that completely would be the "Alice in Wonderland, pie in the sky" type of thinking. I am well aware that in a society where being politically correct and saying the "right thing" (even if one doesn't believe in it or uphold it in one's practice) is valued above facing up to reality, this could be considered as highly controversial and "counter-revolutionary" by some, but lying to ourselves won't bring about any desired change to the world we live in. The reality, as the poet William Wordsworth asserts is that *"the world is too much with us."*

In democracies such as the USA, the issue of campaign finance reform has been a hot topic for decades now, with arguments for and against regulating campaign finance being advanced, but the question from a democratic perspective should be whether limiting the amount of money that one can spend on political advocacy would not be an infringement on people's right to express support for whatever candidate they prefer, given whatever political agenda they want to advance.

Campaign funding is, after all, just another form of lobbying in support of a certain agenda within the context of a democratic contest. Regulation of some sort is necessary to ensure that we don't create a "democracy of the rich" where "he with the most money wins", but it can't be that we approach such an issue with a Black or White, either-or mindset in the world of realpolitik.

Is there any evidence that state resources were used in President Ramaphosa's ascendancy to the ANC presidency, and if not, then what is the fuss all about? An ironic question, if we want to prohibit or limit the usage of money in campaign politics would be, what price do we then put on the right to free speech and expression, which campaign funding is an expression of? There have been no revelations so far of any corruption or corrupt activities by President Ramaphosa and the people who supported him in the campaign, so it would appear that all the fuss just amounts to much ado about nothing.

The better discussion in my view would be how we would seek to advance openness and transparency in both intra and inter-party political contests and political funding to strengthen our democracy, but to take a superfluous, puritanical position on the issue would be highly unrealistic and impractical in my view. English author William Ralph Inge summed it up best when he said that, "it is useless for the sheep to pass resolutions in favour of vegetarianism while the wolf remains of a different opinion."

Liberalism is dead

Ahead of the G20 summit that was recently held in Osaka, Japan, Russian President Vladimir Putin conducted an interview with Financial Times journalists Lionel Barber and Henry Foy, which gave one not just a fascinating insight into the views of one of the most enigmatic characters in the world of international politics but also left one with much food for thought.

Putin's claim that, "the liberal idea has outlived its purpose" and that liberalism has become "obsolete" struck a raw nerve with Western intellectual elites, who have arrogated to themselves the right to tell everyone what is right or wrong within a secular humanist, modern state and was the subject of many opinion pieces in Western capitals, trying to make sense of the conservative advance that is being witnessed across many Western states as ordinary people seemingly reject the supposedly, "enlightened, rational" and more "reasonable" liberal ideal.

One was reminded of a quote by American author and playwright David Mamet, "Liberalism is a religion. Its tenets cannot be proved, and its capacity for waste and destruction is demonstrated. But it affords a feeling of spiritual rectitude at little or no cost." The zeal with which liberals have often dismissed and ridiculed conservative, traditional value systems as "outdated" and "irrelevant" comes to mind here. Liberals have preached the gospel of tolerance and inclusivity, with but one major exception, conservative and traditional, religious views and this is what Putin was "gaaning aan" about.

It wouldn't be too far-fetched to state that the liberal ideal has become the domain of intellectual elites, with their false sense of superiority, whilst ordinary people have remained in the large majority of conservative, traditional leanings, hence the backlash in the Western world. Of course, one could condescendingly attribute this to the lack of education and exposure of the majority in most countries, but that is exactly the kind of arrogance that has led to a populist backlash against liberal ideals in the world we currently live in.

Here in South Africa, we have a unique situation where we have one of the most celebrated constitutions in the world, with high secular humanist, liberal ideals at the forefront, but one could easily argue that the constitution does not truly reflect the conservative values of the mostly black and Afrikaaner majority. It is not an amalgamation of the societal consensus of what values we should espouse as a society, but rather a liberal elite project that is far removed from the ordinary, everyday perspectives of normal South Africans.

One only has to look at the migration debate within South Africa to understand this. Liberals embrace multiculturalism and multi-ethnicity at all costs. But from a migration perspective what about the tensions between the interests of locals versus the rights of migrants? Liberals merely dismiss local interests as xenophobia, and this is the kind of issue that has created a platform for right-wing populism to flourish in the Western world.

A quick survey on the views of most South Africans about the death penalty and what the constitution upholds would once again reveal the critical disjuncture between our liberal, constitutional ideals and what the average South African thinks about the matter. Another pertinent example (being aware of how career limiting this may be, as socialite Zodwa Wabantu and radio DJ Phat Joe have recently found out, as it may be prone to misinterpretation, let me state from the onset that I am pro the rights of the LGBTQI community and am only making this point for illustrative purposes) of the wide gap between liberal ideals and popular value systems in SA, would likely be seen if a survey was conducted on the views of most South Africans about homosexuality in light of our constitutional aspirations.

Is liberalism dead? Of course, not methinks, I mean did God die with Nietzsche's famous proclamation? Are liberal ideals obsolete? Well, did the "end of ideology" really come about because of the fall of the Berlin Wall and the collapse of the doomed Soviet socialist experiment, as most triumphalistic neoliberal scholars believed in the 1990s? What is being reversed however is liberalism's almost messianic claims about what kind of society constitutes the ideal for the best form of human organisation and the constant attacks against traditional institutions such as the church and religious organisations in general.

Young People, The Future Is Now

In his keynote address to the 2010 Mail & Guardian 200 Young South Africans You Must Take to Lunch gathering, Executive Director of the Mapungubwe Institute (MISTRA) and former Head of the Policy Coordination Advisory Unit in the Presidency Joel Netshitenzhe begins by asking the pertinent question: what should be done to ensure that young South Africans in general break free of the psychology of marginalisation?

As we head to the upcoming national elections that are going to be significant in terms of shaping the future of our nation, this is a critical question that needs to be addressed as the youth of South Africa find themselves on the periphery of most political and economic activity within our country. How do we move towards a politics that begins to address the challenge of youth marginalisation in our society?

Firstly, we need to confront the challenge of youth apathy when it comes to involvement in our politics and more specifically to exercising their hard-won right to vote. We need to encourage and mobilise our young people to go out and register to vote and to see their vote as a critical agent of change as we pursue a South Africa that has better social cohesion, greater economic inclusivity, and better opportunities for all, with no strata of society being marginalised as we are currently witnessing.

We need to encourage our youth to adopt the message of hope and renewal for our nation that the Presidency of Cyril Ramaphosa has ushered in, with youth-focused initiatives such as the YES initiative launched by the President in partnership with the private sector and other stakeholders adding further credence to the mantra that youth are the critical role players in shaping our economy and our country. It is the youth of South Africa who must work together to create a better South Africa under the auspices of the #Thuma Mina spirit of President Ramaphosa.

Young people in this country must take hold of the opportunity that the moment we are in presents, to actively participate in the renewal and restoration of our society, in ridding our society of corruption and malfeasance, in fighting unemployment and poverty. All of this means that our youth cannot afford to be passive and disillusioned about the state of our politics. Rather our youth should be at the forefront of the drive for change and a better life for all or in the words of the poet Robert Herrick, "gather ye rosebuds while ye may", carpe diem, seize the day. This means the drive to mobilise young people to register in numbers over the upcoming weekend, should be at the forefront of our priorities as a nation.

In the words of Joel Netshitenzhe from the speech referred to above, "And so my message is a simple one. South Africa stands at the cusp of decision. Whether we tip in the direction of faster progress depends to a large measure on whether we unlock the talent of the nation's youth." Young people have always been at the forefront of all societal change and progress, and it is their energy, creativity, intensity, drive, passion, and ingenuity which remain the great hope of this nation. It is to the youth that we look to in pursuit of a better South Africa, a better continent, and a better humanity.

So, young South Africans must break free of the psychology of marginalisation and actively participate in shaping the future of our country. As part of doing this, we need all our young people to exercise their right to vote and choose the type of leadership that they believe will best serve the interests of the country. To paraphrase the words of the poet Walt Whitman, "The powerful play goes on and you as young people may contribute a verse. "So, young South Africans let us go out there in droves and register to vote over the weekend, because as Joel Netshitenzhe has highlighted, "youth are the leaders of today, not of tomorrow." This is the chance we have to change the present and shape the future for the betterment of the lives of all South Africans

Africa for Africans

Another week has gone by and more drama in our constantly evolving society. Never a dull moment in contemporary SA it would seem, what with the uproar over the brutal rape and murder of a young UCT student followed by violence flaring up once again between South Africans and foreign nationals as they are seemingly called.

I was reflecting on all this and reminded of a trip that I went on with a mate of mine back in 2005, backpacking and hitchhiking through parts of Southern Africa for roughly three months. As one would expect, the trip had many priceless moments: the beauty of Lake Malawi and the species of fish that one sees on a voyage down the lake, the legendary nights at the bar at backpackers' places right across the different countries we visited with overland trucks coming in every day full of European travellers experiencing our beautiful continent.

A midnight drive in a 26-wheeler, 10-gear truck with an Afrikaner oke cold Thys who was driving to Lubumbashi in the Congo and was full of stories of diving for diamonds for the likes of Jonas Savimbi in Angola during his colourful past, rafting and canoeing the Zambezi over two memorable days, finding the most beautiful natural waterfall in some small little village in rural Tanzania, visiting Lusaka in Zambia, the home of the ANC in exile.

Visiting an old missionary church in some mountain of Lake Malawi and spending the night camping there then waking up in the morning and having a near-death experience whilst going down the mountain, almost drowning in Lake Malawi and being rescued by my mate and a German tourist who happened to be sitting across the rocks in some remote part of the Lake. The process of having to bargain for local currency each time we crossed the border into a different country and the funny realities we were confronted with, where my mate who is white would give all the money to me when we crossed the border, but he would be the one swamped by people shouting, "muzungu, muzungu, please give us money"

152

and even though he would tell them that I had the money and not him, they would not believe it because in their eyes it is the white person who must have the money. We always chuckled about that after my mate had managed to frustratingly disentangle himself from these throngs that constantly asked him for money.

The memories are many and the experiences enriching, but what lived longest in the memory was the hospitality of the people in each of the countries we visited, the lasting impression that Africa is a beautiful continent and that we don't travel enough on it. It inspired a commitment to hitchhike and backpack through every continent and write about the experiences before the age of forty, something which one is unfortunately now not going to accomplish. In fact, throughout our trip, my mate and I were the only African people travelling and exploring the continent. The rest were Europeans and North Americans discovering our beautiful continent.

It was heart-warming to arrive in some small towns after midnight and to have locals going out of their way trying to find overnight accommodation for us and ensure we were fine as opposed to looking to rob us. A poignant moment was when we were walking across the border from Zimbabwe to Zambia at Victoria Falls late at night and a posse of young black youths walked past us and greeted us politely. My mate turned to me and said, "You know Mugs, if I was back in SA, I would have been super scared of being robbed when these black youths came past us, but here I never even experienced any fear or anxiety whatsoever." I totally understood what he was saying.

We realised what a violent society we live in as South Africans, how "security conscious" we are as South Africans because of the high levels of crime in our country and what an impediment this is to true freedom.

I was reminded of all this as I was thinking of the unfortunate incidents of violence that broke out in our country this week. These incidents are unfortunate as they are a rejection of African principles of ubuntu and communal living. They are contrary to the warm welcome we received in the eight or so countries we visited during our three months of backpacking and hitchhiking through the southern parts of our lovely continent.

But what is the cause of all this violence I asked? Is it really xenophobia? What are the root causes? I think our fellow Africans are just a convenient scapegoat for our frustrations with our social ills and a social compact that many see as failing them. Rising fuel and transport costs, food prices spiralling out of control, high inflation, cost of living increasing exponentially, no jobs, high inequality with an elite few being perceived to be the true beneficiaries of the democratic dispensation, household income under severe pressure, crime and drugs out of control in communities. State capture and corruption, have curtailed the National Democratic Revolution. These are the real things that South Africans are frustrated about and fighting against, not their fellow African brothers and sisters.

These are the issues that we should be tackling with a sense of urgency as opposed to branding South Africans as unsophisticated, xenophobic, and uncouth criminals.

These are the issues that President Ramaphosa's "New Dawn" must confront head-on and resolve if it is not going to peter out into a false dawn. This requires a new social compact, across all sectors of society to grow South Africa together. Some sacrifices must be made, tough decisions to be taken, and mistakes to be rectified.

The people are not xenophobic or afro-phobic per se. They are hungry, unemployed, frustrated, disappointed, hopeless, and desperate. They need immediate solutions and not more promises and policies. We must acknowledge and deal with this if we are ever to move forward as a people. The solution to all this violence and aggression is found in the famous words of former US President Bill Clinton, "it's the economy, stupid."

ZILLE STRIKES AGAIN

The ghost of GodZille has struck again, with the DA's Helen Zille angering many by tweeting that, if FW De Klerk hadn't dismantled apartheid, "the ANC would still be bogged down in the mess of its so-called liberation camps and infighting. They had no viable armed struggle to speak of" and then putting the nail in the coffin by further adding that, "There are more racist laws today than there were under apartheid".

You don't have to be one of those overrated political analysts that we frequently see on our TV screens, to realise that these two statements are very provocative (deliberately so, one might add) and potentially offensive to many. The least said about the veracity of these statements, the better and others who are much better than me at dissecting and debunking these things have already attempted to do so, hence my focus is on a different aspect arising out of these tweets and the responses they have evoked.

Apart from the expected, "uyas'jwaela uZille" response on social media platforms, many have been very vocal about the fact that they believe that people like Zille should be silenced for having such backward views, that in a democracy such as ours, such stone age views shouldn't be entertained or even allowed room on public platforms.

I found that to be quite interesting, inasmuch as I found the attempt to silence David Bullard a few weeks ago, rather peculiar. Do we shut the likes of Zille and Bullard up for saying things that we may find offensive or disagreeable or do we affirm and defend their right to say those things, whilst at the same time challenging and seeking to expose them on those things on the same public platforms? As an aside, I have always loved Bullard's wit and humour, whilst profoundly disagreeing with his views.

Do we really want to regulate and harass people out of the public space, for holding views that are disagreeable to us, just so that they can retreat into their "laager" and only state those views, which we may believe are prejudiced, at the dinner table or around the braai stand? What is better from a nation-building perspective, to know where you stand with a certain group of people, or to have them pretend publicly because you have pressurised them into political correctness with its innate dishonesty, whilst secretly holding different views?

This is the challenge we are faced with, if we are to succumb to the whims of the "woke" crowd and their impositions on what is correct to say or do within the public space. We know, from platforms such as this one, that there are many white South Africans who think like Zille, who still look down on black people and blackness and assume the worst as a result. We know also, that there are many white people like Zille who believe we owe them for having this modern country with all its infrastructure and hence shouldn't dare complain about colonialism or apartheid.

We know there are many white people who hold to the view that things were much better under apartheid (of course they were for you, duh, because the whole system only catered for you lot in the minority), before the corrupt, inept, useless, "commie" government messed things up. We know there are many white people who see themselves as victims of racism, because of BEE and other such laws, whilst ironically lambasting the "victim mentality" of the black majority as Zille does. Of course, this is all highly contestable, as one could argue that BEE in its origination in SA, was not from a racist black regime as most white South Africans now lament in their victim state(whilst accusing blacks of perpetually playing the victim funny enough), but rather BEE was introduced and supported by the English oligarchs that have dominated the SA economy for so long, during negotiations in the 1980s, as part of a compromise to protect their (white) business interests in the proposed new South Africa at the time.

For them, BEE was the lesser of two evils, given the expectation that the post-liberation "commie" government would nationalise everything and destroy individual enterprise and private ownership. So, we have all these views, that some of us might disagree with vehemently, but if we are to ever become a national democratic society, with non-racialism as one if its core pillars, surely these are some of the views that we must allow to be expressed in the public domain, so we can debunk them and expose them for what they truly are, as opposed to suppressing them under some useless political correctness banner.

In the words of English author Ralph William Inge, "It is useless for the sheep to pass resolutions in favour of vegetarianism, while the wolf remains of a different opinion." What point is there in claiming to be building a non-racial South Africa, when the architects and primary beneficiaries of that racism themselves have not bought into that project and are in fact of a different persuasion, but are forced to suppress their views because it is not politically correct or agreeable to do so?

So, I personally think we have become too soft and sensitive as a society, hence we get offended when the likes of Zille express their admittedly ahistorical and unfactual, inaccurate views, rather than seeing this as an opportunity to set the record straight and publicly expose them for what they truly are. So, we endorse their right to express their warped views, but then aggressively, cogently and compellingly go about breaking down their views on the same public platforms. That is what freedom of expression should mean within a democracy in my view. This is best articulated by English author Evelyn Beatrice Hall when she says, "I disapprove of what you say, but I will defend to the death your right to say it."

We must constantly remind ourselves, when faced with the likes of Zille and their views, of the words of former President Thabo Mbeki, in a famous speech he delivered in 1978 dubbed, The Historical Injustice, "The act of negating the theory and practice of white apartheid racism, the revolutionary position, is exactly to take the issue of colour, race, national and sex differentiation out of the sphere of rational human thinking and behaviour, and thereby expose all colour, race, nation and sex prejudice as irrational.

Our own rational practical social activity, rational in the sense of being anti-racist and non-racist, constitutes such a negation; it constitutes the social impetus and guarantee of the withering away of this irrationality." We must rationally expose the views of people such as Zille, whilst affirming their right to express those views in public, because, at the least, it makes us able to see the "devil" we are dealing with, as opposed to pretensions of being on the same page, whilst back at the ranch we are pulling in opposite directions.

SPRINGBOK COACH JACQUES NIENABER AND ENTRENCHED WHITE PRIVILEGE IN SOUTH AFRICA

With the recent announcement of the Springbok squad for the upcoming 2023 Rugby World Cup, rugby fever has hit the country and in my local watering hole in the north of Johannesburg, the lads have even opened a WhatsApp group specifically to discuss rugby issues, with intense, knowledgeable and very informative debates and discussions about the teams in the various groups of the Rugby World Cup, who are the favourites, squad selection, coaches, playing styles, combinations etc. being par for the course on a daily basis in that group.

Of course, I am uber amped for the Rugby World Cup to start and for the Bokke to once again not only make the nation proud, but contribute positively to the *"gees"* within the country, but a question that has been nagging me consistently in all of this is the following: with a mediocre record of seventeen wins and ten losses in twenty-seven test matches, would Springbok coach Jacques Nienaber have been taking the Boks to the World Cup if he was not part of the Afrikaaner rugby establishment? Does anyone honestly think Nienaber would even have been picked as Bok coach to start with if it were not for the fact that he is entrenched within this rugby *"laager"*? For all those who keep self-righteously and arrogantly telling us to focus on merit within South African society, was Jacques Nienaber even a merit-based selection as Bok coach? I posed these questions on my social media platforms a while back and someone accused me of asking rhetorical questions, hmmmm.

With such an uninspiring record as coach of a World Cup-winning Bok team, why are Nienaber's coaching credentials and pedigree not being questioned as much as say, former Bok coach Pieter De Villiers was, to the point of even denigrating poor old P Div? De Villiers, who also led the Boks to a series victory against the Lions in 2009, just like Nienaber did in 2021, led a Bok team who crucially dominated the All Blacks in the 2009 year, to the point that world rugby felt the need to change the rules in order to neutralise the Bok's ruthless, forward-based power game, which was seen as too boring and predictable for a game which was trying to present itself as a spectacle in order to penetrate new markets and fans.

De Villiers was ridiculed as a mere "token" as Bok coach, as an affirmative action choice who had no right being there, yet Nienaber has received the opposite treatment, being defended by the likes of Swys de Bruin, who claims the Bok winning record under Nienaber is "subjective", that many of the games the Boks have played under Nienaber were mere "trial matches". Former Bok coach Nick Mallet even claimed that the Boks would have won more matches under Nienaber but for some poor refereeing decisions. Why the different treatment for Nienaber when juxtaposed with De Villiers, I have often wondered?

In seeking to answer this question, I was reminded of these words from the brilliant anthology, **Privilege: A Reader, edited by Michael S. Kimmel and Abby L. Ferber**, *"To be white, or straight, or male, or middle class is to be simultaneously ubiquitous and invisible. You're everywhere you look, you're the standard against which everyone else is measured. You're like water, like air. People will tell you they went to see a "woman doctor" or they will say they went to see "the doctor." People will tell you they have a "gay colleague" or they'll tell you about a colleague. A white person will be happy to tell you about a "black friend," but when that same person simply mentions a "friend," everyone will assume the person is white. Any college course that doesn't have the word "woman" or "gay" or "minority" in its title is a course about men, heterosexuals, and white people. But we call those courses* *"literature," "history" or "political science." This invisibility is political."*

At the risk of sounding like those *"Woke"* people who I completely loathe (in my view, *"Woke"* people are the new "moral police", the *"Puritans"* of modern society, a la the character Malvolio in **The Bard's** epic romantic comedy play **Twelfth Night**, and they totally irritate me), one has to say that the difference between the treatment of Pieter De Villiers and Jacques Nienaber as Bok coaches, is simply white privilege. In South African society, with its Eurocentric "centre" to take from **Ngugi Wa Thiong'os Moving the Centre: The Struggle for Cultural Freedoms**, *"Whiteness"* is still associated with competence, capacity, skill, incorruptibility, and ability, whilst *"Blackness"* is reduced to ineptness, corruption, incompetence and being unskilled.

So, a white person in any position in SA society is assumed to be competent, a clean operator, deserving and skilled until they prove otherwise and even when they do, they are defended and excuses are found for them, whilst a black person in any position in SA society is assumed to be incompetent, corrupt, undeserving and unskilled until they prove otherwise, and even when they do, they are still seen as an object of suspicion and ridicule, subjected to what **W.E.B Du Bois** famously *called "double consciousness"* in his the **Souls of Black Folk**. This is why you get the example of Andre de Ruyter, under whose watch Eskom's performance nosedived and since he left performance has dramatically improved, yet *"Whiteness"* in South Africa still sees fit to defend him and blame the *"incompetent, inept, corrupt Black cadres"* for his failure to turn Eskom around. If he had been a black CEO, he would have just been dismissed as another incompetent black, so his failure would have been seen as no surprise whatsoever.

Most black professionals within the corporate world experience this *"double consciousness"* almost daily. This sense of constantly having to evaluate and view yourself from the perspective of *the "other"*, to prove yourself as competent and deserving of *"Whiteness"*, which is the predominant *"centre"* in South African

160

society, as we have not succeeded in moving the centre within the nation (as opposed to between nations) as **Ngugi Wa Thiong'o** enjoins us, despite the fact that we have changed the laws and rules of engagement externally with our highly celebrated Constitution and its Bill of Rights.

This is because putting in place such a progressive Constitution that guarantees rights and freedoms has not changed the fact that South African society remains a highly racialised society with a *"Eurocentric/White centre"* to paraphrase Ngugi and this racialised reality informs and structures a lot of our individual and group experiences, even when we are not necessarily conscious of it. Just read the comments section of most online publications (including this one) if you doubt me okes! Human beings as individuals are constructs of a socialisation process that entails ongoing social interactions, with communication amongst individuals and groups as well as mutual recognition between individuals and groups playing a critical role, so where there is a dominant *"centre i.e Whiteness in this case"* that *"centre"* tends to become the frame of reference or lens through which society gets its values and determines what is success and competence and what isn't (as well as what is corrupt and what isn't one might add, without being defensive of nonsense or degenerating to a logical fallacy).

Is this an unnecessarily racist and provocative analysis? I will let you be the judge of that, but perhaps renowned Nigerian author **Chimamanda Ngozi Adichie** can have the last words in this instance, from her highly acclaimed novel, **Americanah**, *"Race doesn't really exist for you because it has never been a barrier. Black folks don't have that choice."* Maybe it is because of this reality identified by Ngozi Adichie that others in South Africa see white privilege when others are empathically claiming that no such thing exists.

5

MATTERS ARISING

Pricking the Conscience of an Increasingly Amoral Nation

In her book, Ministry of Crime: An Underworld Explored, Mandy Wiener makes the following poignant observation about the state of affairs in South African society, *"corruption is woven into South Africa's social fabric. It is familiar, ubiquitous and sadly deemed acceptable on many levels of society."*

Almost weekly, we hear stories in the news of corruption and corrupt activities implicating top politicians and their associates and it would appear that the phenomenon has now become so prevalent that we have almost become desensitised to it, like Mandy Wiener highlights in the quote above, we have almost resigned ourselves to the reality that corruption is a normal part of our daily, lived reality as South Africans.

Corruption, as we all know, with State Capture being the most pertinent example, is devastating to the life and health of our nation, with government departments, agencies, and entities limping because of corrupt activities by unscrupulous politicians and officials.

In making this astounding, astonishing observation, Mandy Wiener accurately diagnoses one of the biggest problems we are faced with as a country and affirms the fact that contrary to popular belief, corruption is not just a problem of politicians and "ANC people", but rather is a rampant disease that has infected all layers of South African society, hence we have accepted as normal simple things such as the bribing of traffic officials.

The South African disease of corruption is built on another popular South African phenomenon, the love of cutting corners if it'll "make things easier" for us, the "lotto mentality" as I call it, hence the proliferation of get-rich-quick schemes and false prophets and churches promising people instant solutions to their problems.

Former President Thabo Mbeki reflected on this phenomenon in his 2006 Nelson Mandela Memorial lecture when he said, *"Thus, every day, and during every hour of our time beyond sleep, the demons embedded in our society, that stalk us at every minute, seem always to beckon each one of us towards a realisable dream and nightmare. With every passing second, they advise, with rhythmic and hypnotic regularity - get rich! Get rich! Get rich!"*

Of course, corruption is not a uniquely South African or African problem, as our "unreconstructed racist" fellow South Africans have convinced themselves and it is also not a "black government" (read ANC) problem, as "they" (the "unreconstructed racists") also fallaciously, parochially believe. This is not, in any way meant to absolve the ANC-led government of blame for rampant corruption within the state which has almost collapsed service delivery and had a detrimental effect on building state capacity, so don't deliberately get me wrong and label me a corruption apologist here, as you are prone to and are most likely to anyway.

To get a better sense of the facilitatory and complicit nature of other players within society, more specifically the private sector and big, global corporations in rampant corruption within contemporary South Africa, one only has to read the recently released (February 2020) Open Secrets report titled, The Enablers: The Bankers, Accountants, and Lawyers that cashed in on State Capture; or most pertinently the Steinhoff saga.

In reflecting on all of this, one is forced to ask the cliched Leninist question, what is to be done? Firstly, we have to rid ourselves of the false notion which was adopted by secular humanist moderns in the post-Enlightenment era, that human beings are innately good and get corrupted along the way. The converse is true, as so aptly captured by Russian novelist Aleksandr Solzhenitsyn, a man who had profound insights on matters relating to the human condition, having been exposed to the evils of Stalinist Russia, *"If only there were evil people somewhere insidiously committing evil deeds, and it were necessary only to separate them from the rest of us and destroy them. But the line dividing good and evil cuts through the heart of every human being. And who is willing to destroy a piece of his own heart?*

During the life of any heart, this line keeps changing place; sometimes it is squeezed one way by exuberant evil and sometimes it shifts to allow enough space for good to flourish. One and the same human being is, at various ages, under various circumstances, a totally different human being. At times he is close to being a devil, at times to sainthood. But his name doesn't change, and to that name, we ascribe the whole lot, good and evil."

All men are innately corrupt and corruptible as per Solzhenitsyn's assertion. Corruption is a public sector, private sector, and societal problem. Solzhenitsyn reminds us that the fundamental problem of history and humanity is that human beings are innately corrupt and corruptible, contrary to what secular humanist moderns with their intellectual arrogance believe.

The Enlightenment brought to the fore this triumphalistic, humanistic belief in the self-sufficiency and efficacy of human reason and rationality and the belief in the innate goodness of man. Scientific and technological progress has made no impact whatsoever on the condition of the human heart and in wanting to fight corruption successfully, we have to start by dumping the assertion that human beings are inherently good, in line with Solzhenitsyn's thinking and perhaps reconsider "outdated" (in the eyes of moderns) Calvinistic notions of the total depravity of man.

The other people who have it wrong in this regard, are the outdated Marxist-Leninists in our midst, with their dialectical materialism and belief in the altruistic nature of humanity. Friedrich Nietzsche foresaw the dangers of this post-Enlightenment triumphalism of the secular humanists, in his Parable of the Madman (it is very long but profoundly germane in the context of the current discourse),

"Have you not heard of that madman who lit a lantern in the bright morning hours, ran to the marketplace, and cried incessantly: "I seek God! I seek God!" -- As many of those who did not believe in God were standing around just then, he provoked much laughter. Has he got lost? Asked one. Did he lose his way like a child? Asked another. Or is he hiding? Is he afraid of us? Has he gone on a voyage? Emigrated? -- Thus, they yelled and laughed.

The madman jumped into their midst and pierced them with his eyes. "Whither is God?" he cried; "I will tell you. We have killed him -- you and I. All of us are his murderers. But how did we do this? How could we drink up the sea? Who gave us the sponge to wipe away the entire horizon? What were we doing when we unchained this earth from its sun? Whither is it moving now? Whither are we moving? Away from all the sun? Are we not plunging continually? Backwards, sideward, forward, in all directions? Are there still any ups or downs? Are we not straying, as through an infinite nothing? Do we not feel the breath of empty space? Has it not become colder? Is not night continually closing in on us? Do we not need to light lanterns in the morning? Do we hear nothing as yet of the noise of the gravediggers who are burying God? Do we smell nothing as yet of the divine decomposition? Gods, too, decompose. God is dead. God remains dead. And we have killed him.

"How shall we comfort ourselves, the murderers of all murderers? What was holiest and mightiest of all that the world has yet owned has bled to death under our knives: who will wipe this blood off us? What water is there for us to clean ourselves? What festivals of atonement, what sacred games shall we have to invent? Is not the greatness of this deed too great for us? Must we ourselves not become gods simply to appear worthy of it? There has never been a greater deed, and whoever is born after us -- for the sake of this

deed he will belong to a higher history than all history hitherto."

Here the madman fell silent and looked again at his listeners; and they, too, were silent and stared at him in astonishment. At last, he threw his lantern on the ground, and it broke into pieces and went out. "I have come too early," he said then; "my time is not yet. This tremendous event is still on its way, still wandering; it has not yet reached the ears of men. Lightning and thunder require time; the light of the stars requires time; deeds, though done, still require time to be seen and heard. This deed is still more distant from them than most distant stars -- and yet they have done it themselves.

It has been related further that on the same day the madman forced his way into several churches and there struck up his requiem aeternam deo. Led out and called to account, he is said always to have replied nothing but: "What after all are these churches now if they are not the tombs and sepulchres of God?"

So, modernity, with its belief in the goodness of man, and its attack on traditional belief systems and institutions like the family and religion as two examples, totally got it wrong, hence we almost comically, laughably believe that ethics can be taught and inculcated in a course at a business school, or as happened within the Gauteng provincial government recently, where all senior civil servants were required to go through an online ethics course as part of the fight against corruption, through an online module.

In fighting corruption as contemporary South Africans, we have to start by getting rid of this false notion of innate human goodness and move closer towards embracing Calvinistic notions of the total depravity of humanity. This makes corruption not "their" problem (out there), but our collective (there goes that ANC term again, I hear you say) and individual problem as a people. So, from that perspective of understanding innate human corruptibility, we build and uphold institutions and systems at all levels of society that guard against our natural propensity to be corrupt as human beings and we defend and respect those systems and institutions above any political party affiliation, above love and affection for any individual and any ideological biases that we may have. Our democratic checks and balances, our systems and structures should be built with this understanding in mind, not the flawed humanist belief in the inherent goodness of man.

Second, we embrace the fact that ethics and morals (which counter corruption and corruptibility) are inculcated and imbibed in a socialisation process which requires traditional institutions such as family and religion. In other words, these are not outdated institutions, but rather critical pillars of building a healthy, modern society. In the present day, Instagram-influenced South Africa, where the supreme values seem to be materialism (he who has the most toys wins) and hedonism (he who has the most fun and pleasure wins), this focus on socialisation towards a less corruptible society couldn't be more important, because as former President Mbeki said in the Nelson Mandela lecture previously referred to in this piece,

"In these circumstances, personal wealth, and the public communication of the message that we are people of wealth, becomes, at the same time, the means by which we communicate the message that we are worthy citizens of our community, the very exemplars of what defines the product of a liberated South Africa.

This peculiar striving produces the particular result that manifestations of wealth, defined in specific ways, determine the individuality of each one of us who seeks to achieve happiness and self-fulfilment, given the liberty that the revolution of 1994 brought to all of us.

In these circumstances, the meaning of freedom has come to be defined not by the seemingly ethereal and therefore intangible gift of liberty, but by the designer labels on the clothes we wear, the cars we drive, the spaciousness of our houses and our yards, their geographic location, the company we keep, and what we do as part of that company."

In any case, I am not one to moralise and preach to society, these are just the random reflections of an "undeservedly deployed,

Commie, Leftie, inept, incompetent, corrupt ANC cadre", as most on this platform constantly label us.

FRANK TALK WITH BLACK PROFESSIONALS: BLACK MIDDLE CLASS LET US TALK

I have been meaning to write this particular article for the past month and a half or so, after a very enlightening and eye-opening conversation with a mate of mine who is part of our pub group that has been hanging out together at the local watering hole in our neck of the woods in northern Johannesburg for the past decade or so. The said mate is an accomplished black professional and businessperson who gave some very interesting, thought-provoking insights into the psyche of the black middle class in contemporary times, which will form the basis of this entire article.

In light of the recent brouhaha about former PRASA head engineer Daniel Mthimkhulu's fifteen-year conviction by the courts for falsifying his qualifications and the damage that this does to the reputation of black professionals in the eyes of white Saffers (as if it should matter, but that is a conversation you and I will leave for another day) and how this feeds into white arrogance and supremacy as well as fallacious perceptions of black incompetence, ineptness and ineptitude, the timing of this particular piece could not be better in my view, despite having had it in the back of my mind for the past month and a half.

Of course, the irony of it all, without defending the Daniel Mthimkhulu's of this world, is that I know first-hand from my days co-running a recruitment business that focussed mainly on providing black professional candidates to clients within the financial services sector that there are many whites in the corporate sector who have reached the most senior, executive levels, despite being underqualified or not even qualified, but they have been there since the days of apartheid when they were appointed and they now have "experience" and "institutional memory" and now "qualify"(irony of ironies I know right, okes) as skilled and competent.

Anyway, let me leave "uchuku" as my Xhosa mates would say and attend to the matter at hand. My mate whom I mentioned above, is of the view that the current generation of black professionals have a sense of entitlement about where they should be in their careers, ceteris paribus of course. Yes, there are still issues of transformation to reckon with and institutional cultures that prefer "whiteness" over "blackness," but for the purposes of this conversation with black professionals about black professionals, we decided to hold all such variables constant.

From my mate's perspective, there is a lack of urgency and seriousness amongst the black professional and business class about becoming masters at their craft, experts within their field, and the sharpest knife within the set. He spoke about Malcolm Gladwell's highly debated principle, the *"10 000 hour rule"* from his well-known book **Outliers: The Story of Success**, which asserts that in order to become world-class and an expert at any chosen field, one has to dedicate 10 000 hours of hard work, sweat equity and focus to hone one's skills. Of course, the rule itself is not some kind of magical recipe for success, but it is the principle that it espouses that is most important.

In my mate's eyes, when black professionals start off their journey towards building a career and most often seeking to escape poverty by pursuing a formal higher education qualification, they have such a hunger, desire and intensity about them that they are willing to spend hours and hours upon end studying, "swotting" as it were to achieve their objectives. This kind of attitude of learning, grafting and growing is then translated into the workplace once they enter into the field of formal employment, pushing very hard in order to build the ideal life for themselves and achieve their dreams and ambitions, but at some point, when they reach the *"5 000-hour mark"* in terms of the *"10 000 hour rule"* in their careers(and again the principle here is more important than the number), they start to think that they have arrived, they believe that they know much more than they really know and actually see themselves as better professionally than they actually are, which then creates a sense of entitlement and eventually disillusionment with the *"system"*, which is against them (remember, we are still in ceteris paribus mode okes, so don't throw your toys at me just yet please).

So, within this framework, it is between this *"5 000 hours to 10 000 hours"* mark that we lose most black professionals and business people when it comes to becoming experts, industry leaders, top of their field and the system is often blamed unfairly, when it is a waning lack of ambition and focus as well as a false sense of *"having arrived"* and entitlement that is the real problem (again, please hold onto ceteris paribus here fellow darkies, lest we throw the baby out with the bath water). Addressing the Association of Black Securities and Investment Professionals (ABSIP) Conference in November 2016, this is what Joel Netshitenzhe had to say, which is most germane here, *"It is quite apposite that the issue of economic transformation for social change should preoccupy black securities and investment professionals. For, the curse and blessing of history has afforded you and other black professionals the responsibility of thought leadership in the cause of social change. We will all agree that such status cannot be decreed. It depends on self-generated agency: the preparedness constantly to improve the self and the peer group, and to act in a manner that advances social progress."* From *"0 to 5000"* hours, it is easy to work hard and discipline oneself my mate argues, because the motivation is different and oft-times that motivation for darkie professionals is to escape poverty and build a better life for themselves than what they grew up in, but that jump from *"5 000 hours to 10 000 hours"* where one becomes an expert in a particular field, a leader within an industry or sector, a subject matter expert, is much harder than the first *"5 000 hours"* and is often the critical bottleneck for most black professionals. Hmmmm? Food for thought I hear you say or complete bollocks I can hear some of you lot saying, with boiling anger at this *"system darkie"* that is *"speaking from privilege."* Unless we get over labelling, characterisation and "excusology/blameology" (a favourite darkie pastime), we will never have the brutally honest conversations as black people that will assist us to change our developmental trajectory as a people.

In the same speech referred to above, Joel Netshitenzhe makes the salient point that, *"economic transformation for social change should include, but cannot be confined to, the rise of the black elite. Otherwise, it will merely complement white entitlement to historical privilege with black-elite entitlement to larger crumbs that purchase co-optive silence."* Our battle as a nation that is trying to build a culture of winning and success within its people, is against both white entitlement based on historical privilege and also black-elite entitlement based on wanting to sit at the dinner table *"nomakanjani,"* without having truly sweated it out.

Of course, if you lift the ceteris paribus principle, one could dismiss the whole conversation with my mate, this whole article and of course Malcolm Gladwell's *"10 000 hour rule"* as complete drivel and raise legitimate objections about the importance of the environment one operates in, access to resources, social capital, the socio-economic context and other such factors in determining one's success, but methinks there is a more subterranean, brutally honest engagement to be had amongst darkies as it were, when it comes to the subject matter that has informed this article. I will end off with words from a popular 1980s song by the renowned band Sankomota for greater emphasis, *"O phutile matsoho, o shebile banna ha ba sebetsa, Wena..."*

Overcoming the Victimhood Psyche and the Quest for Radical Socio-economic Transformation

It is, as has been the common case over the past decade or so, yet another momentous week in the South African body politic, reminiscent of that famous quote by Vladimir Ilyich Lenin, "There are decades when nothing happens; and there are weeks where decades happen", as former President Jacob Zuma appears before the State Capture Commission.

As the nation is caught in a semi-trance watching the proceedings unfold with Zuma appearing before the Commission, so much of what is happening gives one an insight into the psyche of South Africans, a window into the soul of the so-called Rainbow Nation. President Zuma's well-worn strategy of pleading victimhood, aimed at drawing sympathy from ordinary South Africans more than responding to the pertinent issues that have been raised at the commission, got me thinking about our collective psyche as a people, as a nation.

South African society seems to have embraced a permanent state of victimhood, even to its detriment and hence our leaders and prominent people find it easy to use this against us to advance their narrow agendas. We saw it in the case of Hansie Cronje, caught with his hands "in the cookie jar" and disgraced as a result, but he died as a victimised hero to many who found it easy to sympathise with him. We see it in the seemingly millions of people who support and defend Zuma, seeing him as a victim of mainstream South Africa's racist and classist agenda, despite his many misdeeds. We see it in the black majority, who constantly harp on about the unjust past, to explain their current impoverished status despite being in political power and having the capacity to change the status quo. We see it in the white minority, who cry victim about BEE and EE, despite still being in a position of economic power and privilege.

It is a disease that is prevalent in African society at large, hence we still go to the West with a begging bowl, asking for aid and debt cancellation when we have the mineral and agricultural resources that are critical to the functioning of the global economic system. So, a critical first step in moving from a deconstructionist to a constructionist "African Agenda" and decolonising our economies, within the global political realm requires that we disabuse ourselves of this victimhood psyche. It is a necessary step in the evolution of the African struggle as we seek to increasingly assert ourselves in the 21st century.

This took me to the thinking of a brilliant 20th-century thinker,

Reinhold Niebuhr, whose collectivised philosophical outlook is captured in one of his quotes, "evil is not to be traced back to the individual, but to the collective behaviour of humanity." As renowned American ethicist Dr Lisa Sowle Cahill hypothesises, according to Niebuhr, "the task of the community, in the interim, then, is neither self-reliant action nor patient resignation, but a sort of quiet preparation- a creation of the conditions of real construction."

Niebuhr believed that profound change in the world we live in would not come about without occasions of destruction taking place. So, in pursuit of the radical socio-economic transformation (not the political red-herring of Zuma's RET crew) that is an existential necessity for building the type of inclusive and equitable South Africa that most reasonable South Africans would like to see, we have to be brave enough to take steps that will lead to the destruction of the current system with all its idiosyncrasies unless we want to perpetuate cycles of inequality and exclusion that produce a permanent state of inertia through a victimhood psyche.

This touches on critical issues of restitution and historical redress, necessary preconditions for growing our country together, that must be imposed as opposed to taking a laissez-fair approach that is characteristic of a disempowered, victimhood state of being. Reinhold Niebuhr himself was highly cynical about the power of appeals to human-fellow feelings to bring about great transformations. In his eyes, real social change could only occur if there were adjustments in the balance of power, forcibly so if needs be. This is the type of stuff that a society with a victimhood mindset would never embark on. Of course, it bears highlighting Niebuhr's thinking was utilitarian, in that the outcome would be long-term societal good, a movement towards the desired national democratic society in the South African context.

So, we need to move to shed the victim mentality if we are ever going to grow our country together in a manner that produces a better South Africa for all. We need to prove the bona fides of our young democracy, by taking bold steps to resolve all the problems that we have inherited, as opposed to seeing ourselves as passive recipients/victims of consequences for historical actions which we had no control over. As Reinhold Niebuhr himself stated, "Democracy is finding proximate solutions to insoluble problems."

Robert Mugabe and Africa's Historical Revisionism

The passing away of former Zimbabwean President Robert Mugabe has led to much debate about his legacy, with people on both extremes either reviling him as a brutal murderer and typically despotic African dictator or lauding him as a liberator ala Simon Bolivar and profoundly committed African nationalist who did much to advance the African's cause for complete emancipation from colonial era shackles and the devastating consequences therein that are still to a large extent felt and experienced in Africa even in this present day.

The popular misperception seems to be that Mugabe was a good guy who went rogue, that he started very well and only veered towards the dark side when he started with the much-maligned "land grabs" as part of his land reform policy. This is a view that many in the West even hold up to today and is borne out by the fact that the British knighted him at some point, only reversing that decision a couple of decades later. It is quite an interesting and insightful outcome when one looks at the global balance of power, that for all that he had done before, Mugabe was considered a "good guy" until he made the mistake of touching white interests in Zimbabwe, then he started being seen as the epitome of evil, but that is a debate for another day. You don't have to like it or acknowledge it, but it is what it is as they say.

Was Robert Gabriel Mugabe a good guy turned bad? When looking at anyone's legacy, will simplistic distinctions between good and evil ever suffice given the innate condition of the human heart if one were to follow Calvinistic theological dogma? My view, on the issue of good and evil, as I have stated before is aptly and succinctly captured by the perspective of Russian novelist Aleksandr

Solzhenitsyn in his haunting reflections on the brutal realities of Stalinist Russia in his book, The Gulag Archipelago. Would that we could just simplify life, meaning and existence to the distinction of good and bad guys when analysing human society and history, but alas those who are honest about resolving such conundrums often find the issue to be a tad more complex than that.

Now for me, the issue of Mugabe's legacy has been one of great interest, given that I was named after the bloke and have had to spend my entire life trying to explain the reason for that whenever I enter any new space. Of course, the fact I was named after him placed a heavy burden on me over the years to study the man, his life, and his impact and to find some kind of posture about him that I could stand on for myself.

It has been interesting (and hilarious) over the years each time I meet new people, to hear responses like, "Aag shame, why would your parents do that to you?" Or other typical responses after I introduce myself like, "Are you related?" (No). "Are you from Zim?" (No). "Don't you think it would be better if you change your name to something better?" (No). I always laugh all of this off and tell people that I never have any awkward moments when I meet new people, because by the time I have tried to explain my name and been the butt of a few jokes based on it, the ice has already been broken and the conversation is already flowing with some kind of familiarity. See, you can always find a positive in any negative folks.

I maintain that the biggest lesson of my late dad naming me after Robert Mugabe is that you should never name your child after a so-called hero who is still alive, because he or she still has time to reverse that legacy which makes his or her contemporaries see him or her as a hero. In any case, on issues such as this, my view has always been that the judgement of posterity must hold greater weight than that of contemporaries.

Reflecting on Mugabe's legacy leaves one with much food for thought and is made even more complicated by the fact that Africans insist on religiously holding on to the principles behind the

Latin phrase, "De mortuis nil nisi bonum" (of the dead, say nothing but good). This means that we are inclined to historical revisionism whenever we look back at the legacy of someone we considered great or who was prominent during their times.

To be fair, Mugabe did do well in his initial years leading Zimbabwe in terms of his education policies and his handling of the economy, with the hyperbolic cliché of Zimbabwe having been the "breadbasket of Africa" being put forward as evidence for that. He did present himself as a reconciler ala Mandela, who would guarantee the protection of the interests of the white minority in the initial years. But does all this then present evidence of a man who started as a "good guy" but ended up deviating towards "evil"?

My take is that even that popular narrative about Mugabe is false. He has always been a violent, brutal individual atop a violent, brutal political formation, ZANU. He did not suddenly become "evil" when he supposedly "turned" on the white minority in Zimbabwe in the 1990s. His conduct then was consistent with his politics right throughout his career, and it was only because this brutality was finally being unleashed on white Zimbabweans in the 1990s that the international community finally stood up and started to characterise him as "evil". From being a man worthy of being knighted by the crown, he was now reduced to the caricature "Mad Bob."

Mugabe's history of brutality is seen in how he engineered a prison coup, to remove ZANU's founding leader Ndabaningi Sithole from leadership and how he treated Sithole from therein till his death in 2000. Following on from that, we see it in the assassination and murder of ZANU's leader in exile at the time, Herbert Chitepo who was in exile in Zambia. Both occurrences paved the way for Mugabe's unilateral ascendance to power within ZANU. In fact, even though a former Rhodesian Central Intelligence official wrote a biography in which he claimed that they were responsible for Chitepo's assassination, it is telling that a commission of inquiry initiated by former Zambian President Kenneth Kaunda found that

Chitepo's death was due to internal infighting and jostling for power within ZANU at the time.

The historically consistent brutality of Mugabe and ZANU can also be seen in the mysterious death of war hero, Josiah Tongogara, killed in a highly suspicious accident on the way to Mozambique to inform the troops that the war was over. Tongogara, a former commander of ZANU's military wing ZANLA, was seen as a moderate during the Lancaster House conference who favoured cooperation and unity between Mugabe's ZANU and Joshua Nkomo's ZAPU. He was a popular war hero who in some circles, was seen as a direct rival to Mugabe in a post-independence Zimbabwean state.

We see this brutality even more eerily in the events of Gukurahundi and the Matabeleland massacres and in contemporary times in the mysterious death by "accident" (a fire in his house) of another war hero Rex Nhongo AKA Solomon Mujuru, who made the mistake of defying Mugabe and lost his life for it as a result, albeit through a supposed "accident." I hope you can now see that the popular narrative of Mugabe being a good guy gone bad is profoundly historically inaccurate.

Mugabe's legacy leaves room for many more debates. For example, his land reform policy, which though necessary to fix a historical injustice (and I know many readers won't like this point) was executed in a rather clumsy and highly corrupt, inept manner. Mugabe's land reform policy raises a question that remains highly germane and unresolved in contemporary times on the continent: can a historically unjust act (the stealing of land) become constitutionally justifiable owing to the passage of time?

His anti-imperialist stance for which he is highly celebrated on the continent, raises other questions and issues for contemporary Africans. How should we, as ordinary Africans respond, when corrupt, despotic and selfish leaders use anti-imperialist rhetoric as a red herring to prevent us from scrutinising their nefarious activities? This can be seen in SA in the Zuma-era "White monopoly capital" ruse as well as in one of the main opposition party's populist rantings whenever their leader's conduct and ethics are questioned.

Mugabe's legacy as a Pan-Africanist is highly questionable. One would even question whether Mugabe should be considered an ideologue who tried to advance any ideology at all. The closest thing that Mugabe believed in, which could be called an ideology at a stretch, can be found in his own words, "our votes must go together with our guns. After all, any vote we shall have shall have been the product of the gun. The gun which produces the vote should remain its security officer- its guarantor. The people's votes and the people's guns are always inseparable twins." So, if the people's vote goes against us, we have our guns, violence, intimidation, and murder to keep ourselves in power. This is Mugabe and ZANU at their best, not just post the 1990s as the popular narrative holds, but right throughout their history, as long as Mugabe and his ilk were at the helm.

So, in bidding farewell to a man whose life and politics have defined an era for Africa, we would do well to remind ourselves of the words of the poet Percy Bysse Shelley in the poem Ozymandias, "My name is Ozymandias, king of kings; Look on my works, ye mighty and despair!"

The Winnie Mandela We Know and Love

The passing away of struggle icon and "Mother of the Nation", Mam Winnie Madikizela Mandela has led to many comments and reflections on her legacy which are profoundly germane for us in terms of where we are as a nation and where we aspire to be.

Mam Winnie Madikizela Mandela was a lifelong crusader for freedom, social justice, equality, inclusivity, and a more equitable South African society but despite that fact, her legacy is highly debated depending on which side of the spectrum you fall in.

We have seen how others have tried to reduce her contribution to the anti-Apartheid struggle to merely being former President Nelson Mandela's wife, a total distortion of her immense contribution to our people's struggle for freedom.

Mam Winnie was able to carve a niche for herself as a true liberator of our people, independent of any relationship that she had with former President Nelson Mandela, and it is because of the great sacrifices made by people like her that we enjoy the freedoms that we do in contemporary South Africa.

She was an advocate of the rights of women, but she wasn't just a leader of women but South African society, hence the great outpourings of love and appreciation all over the country since the news of her passing away was announced earlier this week.

She was a leader that ordinary South Africans could easily identify with because in the days of the anti-apartheid struggle right into our new democracy, she was always on the ground with the people, advocating for their issues and fighting for the rights of those who are marginalised, who are on the periphery, the subalterns of this country that we are still in the process of building.

She was a radical, militant revolutionary whom the youth of South Africa, one of the most marginalised demographics in this democracy of ours, could always identify with and look up to. Hence, she was one of the only defendants of the militant post-2011 Gallagher Estate ANC YL generation which called for land expropriation without compensation and the nationalisation of mines and all the natural resources of the country.

She was also one of the key inspirations for the #Fees Must Fall generation which shook up the country a couple of years ago. All these young people looked up to her and got inspiration from her because their fight for economic emancipation and greater access to education and opportunity was a struggle to which she dedicated her life and never compromised.

Unlike Nelson Mandela and other ANC leaders who are eulogised and deified as if they had no flaws, she was a fallible, flawed heroine whom all of us as ordinary South Africans could easily

180

identify with. She bore the brunt of the apartheid government's brutality along with ordinary South Africans, who are the true heroes of our struggle and spent her life as a leader amongst the people, her struggle being their struggle and hence she has an unparalleled standing amongst the people of this country. Contrary to what those who criticise her legacy want us to believe, it is her fallibility that is indeed one of her most endearing qualities for us ordinary South Africans.

The fact that some of her flaws are openly highlighted whilst those of other leaders who were prominent in the struggle are swept under the carpet speaks to the fact that we live in a patriarchal society, where different standards are applied for male and female leaders, a hypocritical stance that we as a country need to rid ourselves of.

The constant attempt to portray her as tainted, whilst deifying the likes of Nelson Mandela speaks to this double standard that our society has adopted. It is this double standard that we need to challenge, a standard that openly accepts and celebrates a Nelson Mandela but on the other side isolates and problematizes a Winnie Mandela. This is a struggle that most black South Africans in various sectors of society are faced with daily, where our successes and our achievements are constantly questioned and downplayed. So once again, Mam Winnie's struggle was and is our daily struggle.

In reflecting upon the impact that this great woman had on the life and soul of this nation, one is reminded of the brilliant poem Oh Me! Oh Life by Walt Whitman, *"Oh me! Oh life! Of the questions of these recurring,*

Of the endless trains of the faithless, of cities fill'd with the foolish,

Of myself forever reproaching myself, (for who more foolish than I, and who more faithless?)

Of eyes that vainly crave the light, of the objects mean, of the struggle ever renew'd,

Of the poor results of all, of the plodding and sordid crowds I see around me,

Of the empty and useless years of the rest, with the rest of me intertwined,

The question, O me! so sad, recurring—What good amid these, O me, O life?

Answer.

That you are here—that life exists and identity,

That the powerful play goes on, and you may contribute a verse."
Indeed, she contributed a great verse in this "great play" of building a better South Africa and we are all permanently indebted to her and those whom she spent a large part of her life fighting alongside with for the emancipation of our people. Lala ngoxolo Mam Winnie Madikizela Mandela.

Mother tongue education in South Africa

Mother tongue education is a strategic, long-term imperative for a country with a diverse and rich cultural heritage like South Africa, coming from a divided past where certain languages and people groups were given preference over others in an unjust and unfair manner. To mention this point is not to be "over-emotional", but rather to show an understanding and appreciation of the importance of ridding this country of its apartheid legacy and the colonial structure of its society.

To be sure, this will require huge investment and re-allocation of resources, but the benefits on a long-term basis of promoting our diversity and building our "Rainbow Nation" by developing all our languages, which in the end safeguard, develop and modernise our cultures, will far outweigh the costs if such an exercise wasn't undertaken. After all, cost and level of difficulty can never be used as a valid reason for refusing to undertake activities of particular strategic significance to the health and well-being of a nation.

Languages and cultures develop as the people within a certain language group and culture become more economically affluent (e.g. Afrikaners in South Africa), so as part of the broader goal of transforming South African society and giving the African majority a greater say in the running of the country's economy, we have to find a way to develop African languages by teaching kids in their home languages from an early age onwards.

In his Moving the Centre: the Struggle for Cultural Freedoms, Ngugi wa Thiong'o argues this quite cogently and in fact he asserts that, *"for a full comprehension of the dynamics, dimensions and workings of a society, any society, the cultural aspects cannot be seen in total isolation from the economic and political ones. The quantity and quality of wealth in a community, the manner of its organisation from production to the sharing out, affect, and are affected by the way in which power is organised and distributed. These in turn affect and are affected by the values of that society as embodied and expressed in the culture of that society. The wealth and power and self-image of a community are inseparable."*

Ngugi further argues that the battle to move the centre from a Eurocentric worldview to one that recognises and affirms local culture(s) and tradition(s), within the context of a universalist approach that is appreciative of the fact that all cultures are evolutionary and are in fact constantly being influenced by interactions and exposure to other cultures, is one that entails moving the centre "between nations and within nations", because of our colonial past, which has created societies which are dominated and subjugated by the Eurocentric worldview.

It is within this context that the struggle for mother tongue education becomes an existentialist revolutionary imperative for a nation such as ours with its rich diversity. As Ngugi states, *"hence the need to move the centre from all minority class establishments within nations to the real creative centres among the working people in condition of gender, racial and religious equality."*

A discussion of this nature is germane within our current political discourse, especially as we celebrated World Teacher's Day on the

05th of October 2022, with the Minister of Basic Education, in honouring this day, re-affirming government's commitment to change the language policy in the country in order to make education accessible to all, in line with the Basic Education Laws Amendment (BELA) Bill and the National Curriculum Statement (NCS) Grades one to twelve, which is about the enablement of the equal use of all eleven languages, including sign language, in the basic education schooling system. This is of course a right that is enshrined in the constitution, as per Section 29(2) of the Bill of Rights.

Promoting our African languages in this manner is critical to enabling the African majority to develop themselves educationally as well as in the fields of science, technology and innovation, as these languages themselves will have to develop a conceptual vocabulary that is commensurate with modernity and its advances in science and technology. It is also important in doing what Ngugi calls "decolonising the imagination", a necessary precondition to enabling Africans within our society to contribute meaningfully in the crucial economic development field of innovation as well as contributing to the creative arts, which are at the heartbeat of stimulating the creative energy and entrepreneurial spirit that are at the heartbeat of the upward economic mobility of any group of people(s) within any society. Non-racialism and multiculturalism are also enhanced and advanced through promoting mother tongue education within the broader ambit of building our aspirant "Rainbow Nation".

Blacks Must Just Build Their Own Stuff

Judge Sisi Khampepe has just delivered a report, after an inquiry was commissioned by Stellenbosch University, to investigate allegations of racism against the institution, when an Afrikaner student was filmed urinating on the study desk of a Black, African student earlier this year and this went viral and after that, during October, another Afrikaner student urinated inside the room of two Black students. All of this rightfully caused an uproar, with Black students openly calling for an end to racial discrimination at Stellenbosch University.

In accepting the outcomes and recommendations of the Judge Khampepe report, Stellenbosch vice-chancellor Wim de Villiers openly acknowledged that there are indeed racial problems within Stellenbosch University, with most Black students and academics expressing sentiments and lived experiences of being unwelcome and unaccepted at the institution and he has committed the university to take action to rectify and remedy this, in line with recommendations from the Khampepe report.

I was reflecting on all this and just thinking to myself, "Why the heck do darkies not just build their own institutions and stop subjecting themselves to all this?" Twenty-eight years into democracy, we should surely have been able to build African language schools and tertiary institutions that are centres of excellence in preserving, developing, and promoting African cultures in this country as well as primary custodians and enablers of the decolonisation and transformation of South African society.

To quote the words of Ngugi wa Thiong'o, *"Language as communication and culture are then products of each other. Communication creates culture, culture is a means of communication. Language carries culture, and culture carries, particularly through orature and literature, the entire body of values by which we come to perceive ourselves and our place in the world. How people perceive themselves affects how they look at their culture, at their politics and at the social production of wealth, at their entire relationship to nature and to other beings. Language is thus inseparable from ourselves as a community of human beings with a specific form and character, a specific history, a specific relationship to the world."*

In my view, instead of trying to *"de-Afrikanerise"* tertiary institutions such as Maties and Tukkies or schools such as Affies and Grey Bloem, Blacks should be building their own, African language tertiary institutions and schools, which are just as excellent, if not even more, and which can advance the transformation agenda much more effectively and efficaciously than what we are currently witnessing.

I mean, of course, there should be no aspect of South African society which is exclusive to advancing the language and culture of a certain people group, to the extent of being discriminatory against people from other ethnicities who may want to immerse themselves in that culture, but there should be nothing wrong with an institution being clear that it is built to advance, develop, and promote a certain culture (including Afrikaans folks), obviously within the broader ambit of nation-building and aspirant *"Rainbow Nationism"*.

Ngugi wa Thiong'o argues that African governments should deliberately, systematically include African languages in learning institutions as a mode of preserving, developing, and promoting African cultures and I would take the argument even further and say that within South Africa, the government should be building and developing African language schools and tertiary institutions, to the extent that they also become globally competitive centres of excellence, research, knowledge production, sporting excellence, and cultural as well as economic advancement, the same way this has been done by the likes of Maties and Tukkies et al for the Afrikaans culture and its people.

Ultimately, the end goal is to make African languages also languages of commerce, as Africans themselves become more affluent and upwardly mobile economically, because in truth unless a language can become a language of commerce, there is no incentive for anyone to study using it. After all, whatever output they produce using that language will not be able to assist them to advance economically. Of course, this is a chicken and egg situation in light of the argument that I am endeavouring to advance within this piece.

Not too long ago, Solidarity built a whole tertiary institution to advance Afrikaner interests, Sol-Tech Technical Training College in Pretoria, with a budget of R300 million, but it was built under budget and finished even earlier than planned nogal. Solidarity accomplished this using monthly contributions from their members, which begs the question for me, with all these organisations that have been formed to supposedly advance transformation for the benefit of the Black majority in South Africa in existence, what is preventing we darkies from doing a similar thing? Why can't we just build our stuff and in doing so bring about a real transformation of South African society?

Without the development of African languages, African cultures will become even more marginalised and at greater risk of going the way of the dodo and the quagga within our society and without the different cultures, our diversity as a people is lost and all pretensions of *"Rainbow Nationism"* are exposed as mere *"Alice in Wonderland"* type fantasies. To quote Ngugi wa Thiong'o again, *"If you know your mother tongue and add it with all other languages, that is empowerment"* or as Frantz Fanon so aptly and succinctly puts it, *"to speak a language is to take on a world, a culture."*

National Development: Planning Over Populism, Ideas Over Ideology

Whilst reading President Cyril Ramaphosa's recent weekly article to the nation, bemoaning the country's collapsing public infrastructure and its negative impact on service delivery, a few things came to mind as I reflected on the President's very sobering words. Firstly, why are we failing to utilise industry bodies within the infrastructure and built environment space to improve government's maintenance and delivery of public infrastructure? These are industry bodies such as Consulting Engineers South Africa (CESA), Council for the Built Environment (CBE), South African Quality Institute (SAQI), South African Institution of Civil Engineering (SAICE), South African Council for the Property Valuers Profession (SACPVP), Engineering Council of South Africa (ECSA),

Green Building Council South Africa (GBCSA), South African Council for the Architectural Profession (SACAP), Chartered Institute of Building (CIOB), South African Council for Project and Construction Management Professionals (SACPCMP), which have the technical skills and know-how to not only compliment but improve government's infrastructure delivery and maintenance outcomes.

What about sitting down with organisations such as the Southern African Venture Capital and Private Equity Association (SAVCA) along with various development finance institutions to bring bankable, shovel-ready projects to the table that can be financed through innovative financing products and mechanisms, as part of building transformative public-private partnerships that have a developmental thrust? I was reminded of a conversation that I had a couple of weeks ago with a friend of mine from my varsity days, who is the CEO of one of these built environment and infrastructure development industry bodies and they were expressing to me how sad it is for them that government is not galvanising the technical and project management skills within some of these bodies as part of its drive to improve infrastructure project delivery and maintenance.

I was also reminded of a book I read not too long ago, titled From Third World to First - The Singapore Story:1965-2000, a book which summarises Singapore's transmogrification from an inconsequential, underdeveloped Third World country to currently being so developed and industrialised that it ranks fourth amongst the world's most competitive economies, it is a manufacturing hub with a booming services sector, it is ranked second after Switzerland on the list of least risky countries to invest in, it is the most digitally competitive economy in Asia and boasts the best global smart city. In short, Singapore is a strong, dynamic, resilient economy that South Africa can learn from, as we seek to resolve some of our stubborn developmental challenges and move from developing to developed world status ourselves.

From the book, I got to interact with the thinking of Lee Kuan Yew, who is accredited with taking his country Singapore, the smallest in

South East Asia and with a limited supply of natural resources (unlike South Africa) from being highly underdeveloped to being developed and who led them through a tremendous growth spurt economically, diversifying their economy to the extent that Singapore developed to the powerhouse that it is today economically.

Firstly, I was intrigued by Lee Kuan Yew's emphasis on the importance of long-term planning over populism in pursuit of national development and ideas as well as innovation over being dogmatic and an ideologue. Interestingly enough, he was not a big fan of a copy-and-paste approach to national development, as much as he believed that one could learn from those who have succeeded, as in his view each nation has to build its institutions in pursuing a developmental path, in line with the cultural ethos of its people, as opposed to merely importing or having western norms imposed on it. In fact, in his view, the Americans and the West were just as bad as the Communists in trying to shove their way of doing things down the throats of the developing world, like an article of faith. In his own words, *"after the end of the Cold War, the U.S. became as evangelical as the communists. It is an article of faith. I mean, democracy, human rights, free flows of capital -- it does not brook a counter-argument. They believe this is right, and therefore let's do it. I think there's a certain overwhelming belief that what's worked for America will work worldwide and that this way the world will be a better place."* As a party man himself, having been the Secretary-General of the governing People's Action Party in Singapore between 1954 and 1992 and leader of his country from 1959 to 1990, he was of the view that in pursuit of national development aspirations for your country, you have to fight off the ideologues, the fanatics within your party and he used Deng Xiaoping in China as an example of someone who did this. Pragmatism over proselytising was his preference, as Deng Xiaoping himself preached in turning China around.

Whilst he highlighted the importance of building institutions in pursuit of national development, in his view, local customs and culture must be incorporated into building these institutions, to be successful. Interestingly enough for me, there's a point where he talks about the importance of decisive, strong, visionary leadership, almost insinuating that even the imposition of democracy and its Western norms in a developing country, can be counterdevelopmental. One of the biggest Western criticisms of his decades of leading Singapore towards the promised land of economic prosperity is that he was autocratic.

Here's what Lee Kuan Yew himself had to say on the matter, *"When you have a popular democracy, to win voices you have to give more and more. And to beat your opponent in the next election, you have to promise to give more away. So, it is a never-ending process of auctions—and the cost, the debt being paid for by the next generation. Presidents do not get re-elected if they give a hard dose of medicine to their people. So, there is a tendency to procrastinate, to postpone unpopular policies in order to win elections. So, problems such as budget deficits, debt, and high unemployment have been carried forward from one administration to the next."* As if to say that there's a point where democracy itself may be a bottleneck, an impediment to national development and a true statesman (as opposed to a mere leader) ought to rise above these popular democracy tendencies in pursuance of development for their nation. Hmmm, but that is a subject for another day.

He loathed communism as something which history has shown does not work, and preferred market economy fundamentals and encouraging competitiveness as a basis for developing a country's economy and he referenced many of his contemporaries who had gone on a Marxist-Leninist journey of trying to build their countries at around the same time as him, one of whom was Mwalimu Julius Nyerere, of whom he had this to say, *"Oh, yes, Julius Nyerere was a good Christian. He wanted to do good to his people. He was a great Christian; he could quote you chunks of the Bible. He was a preacher also. He was a devout Catholic. But he didn't understand the economics of growth or just simple economics. He thought if you gather people together -- I think it's called "ujamaa," or some* form of communalised agriculture. So he had them all in villages, and they would work their farms. And then they were living together, and the children would go to school, and you can provide health services and so on. These are noble objectives. But walking back and forth to your farm, there's nobody to look after them and so on, and then you have cooperatives that buy the products at uncompetitive prices, so the whole thing malfunctions. It was a terrible waste." For Lee Kuan Yew, a mixed economy model with market fundamentals, but with the state driving and directing the economy was preferable, not this either/or polarised thinking about economic development that many fall prey to.

Interestingly enough for us in South Africa with National Health Insurance being such a topical issue, he talks about having been in England as a student in the 1940s and how they passed the National Health Service Act, giving free healthcare to the population. It almost went broke, and they eventually ended up having to put some kind of prescription charge.

In his view, such kind of a national health scheme is ineffective and inefficient, and he says the English have kept it because it is now part of the national psyche and too popular, but it is inefficient, as can be evidenced by the long queues for basic medical services. From his perspective, the state must subsidise health, it must subsidise education and housing as these are basics that need to be guaranteed if you want people to perform effectively in order to successfully build a nation.

So, he says subsidise certain basic services, but don't offer them for free, as that automatically leads to waste (buffet syndrome as he calls it, people utilise more than they need) and people don't truly value anything that they have not put in something for, as money is a symbol of value in the modern world. South Africa, with all its basic developmental challenges such as failure to adequately deliver and maintain public infrastructure, leading to manifold service delivery hiccups and backlogs, can learn a thing or two from the thinking of Lee Kuan Yew methinks.

ABOUT THE AUTHOR

Mugabe Ratshikuni is a writer, columnist, thought-leader, opinion-maker, scholar, entrepreneur, social activist, and civil servant. He holds a Bachelor of Arts majoring in Philosophy, Politics and Economics and a Bachelor of Arts Honours in International Politics. He is currently employed by the Gauteng Department of Human Settlements as Director: Policy and Research.

www.ingramcontent.com/pod-product-compliance
Lightning Source LLC
Chambersburg PA
CBHW072141270326
41931CB00010B/1843